"This book distils many years of professional negotiation experience – it simply works."
Jochen Rink, Director, Department of Tissue Dynamics and Regeneration, Max Planck Director

"A must-read book that offers a blueprint for handling conflicts, negotiating partnerships and concluding lasting agreements. It provides practical guidance and uses engaging stories. As a professional with an impressive track record in successful negotiations, Melissa Davies expertly introduces her solution-focused approach. She offers a five-step guide to lasting agreements, enlivened by real-life examples from business, politics and humanitarian action. A compelling, highly accessible and timely book that will change your negotiation mindset and skills."
Frédéric Varone, Professor of Political Science, University of Geneva

"*The Practical Negotiation Handbook* offers a fresh take on negotiations. Melissa Davies emphasizes a constructive and collaborative approach aimed at building long-term partnerships. The book offers extremely practical, easy-to-implement advice on getting what you want from a negotiation. She focuses on hard skills and tactics – as you would expect from a book on negotiations – but also helps to develop the soft skills needed to land a good deal and build a long-term relationship at the same time."
Lynda Mansson, Director General, MAVA Foundation

"Caution! This book could fundamentally change how you think about negotiation. Taking advantage of her extensive experience in partnerships building, Melissa Davies gives us a thorough and handy guide to bringing out the best in our negotiations and achieving sustainable collaborations. You will find this book fascinating, and your counterpart will be delighted that you have read it. I loved Melissa's very simple and rigorous approach. It was interesting to put it in perspective with what we teach at university:

both we (based on scientific studies) and Melissa (based on her experience) arrive at very similar conclusions. Does this mean that for once theory and practice meet?"
Lisa Faessler, PhD candidate in Management and assistant for Negotiation classes, University of Lausanne

"Incredibly helpful! *The Practical Negotiation Handbook* is indeed what the title says, providing a very useful and elegant five step model for 'solution-focused negotiation'. It describes in practical detail a process where each negotiating party explores the conditions under which they could say yes to the other party's request. There are plenty of gems here – online negotiations, non-violent communication, mindset, non-cognitive skills, multicultural negotiation. And a really insightful chapter on gender and negotiation including gender backlash and the influence of race and culture on gender, further developed out with the author's own experience as a negotiator over 25 years."
Tim Newton, Sustainability Manager, Solution Focused Practitioner, UKASFP

"I've been applying Melissa's life-changing approach to negotiation on work and personal projects, and it has done wonders to establish the best outcome in any situation. I would recommend this read to all my friends and co-workers."
Sandra Pichon, Engineering Director, Nagravision

"I consider negotiation a key survival skill that can be learned and practiced continuously to achieve more in life and at work, now and in the future. Melissa's book is very easy to read and I agree with her that "the best indicator of a successful negotiation is its sustainability. Melissa establishes interesting links with the solution focused coaching methodology and explores some original angles, like gender diversity or the challenges related to remote communication in critical conversations. Enjoy the read!"
Ofra Hazanov, Head of Talent & Development, EPFL (Swiss Federal Institute of Technology Lausanne)

"A systemic view of negotiation with clear procedures and helpful examples. I can now prepare myself for negotiations in a completely different way and I know to respond much better to my counterpart."
Caroline Biewer, Team Lead HR Development and Training, Helsana

"A very good read. I particularly like how the author clearly distinguishes between negotiations and other means of reaching a solution, and discusses under which circumstance either have their justification."
Gerlind Wallon, Deputy Director, EMBO

The Practical Negotiation Handbook

A five-step approach to lasting partnerships

Melissa Davies

KoganPage

First published in Great Britain and the United States in 2021 by Kogan Page Limited

2nd Floor, 45 Gee Street
London
EC1V 3RS
United Kingdom
www.koganpage.com

122 W 27th St, 10th Floor
New York, NY 10001
USA

4737/23 Ansari Road
Daryaganj
New Delhi 110002
India

© Melissa Davies 2021

ISBNs

Hardback   978 1 3986 0182 6
Paperback   978 1 3986 0180 2
Ebook   978 1 3986 0181 9

British Library Cataloguing-in-Publication Data

A CIP record for this book is available from the British Library.

Library of Congress Cataloging-in-Publication Data

Names: Davies, Melissa, author.
Title: The practical negotiation handbook: a five-step approach to lasting
    partnerships / Melissa Davies.
Description: London; New York, NY: Kogan Page, 2021. | Includes
    bibliographical references and index. | Summary: "Effective negotiations lead to sustainable partnerships, help both parties to achieve higher goals than they would alone and allow organizations to avoid the costly price of conflict. This book outlines a simple and powerful method of negotiating, either in person or virtually. The Practical Negotiation Handbook outlines a tried and tested five-step process for negotiating lasting agreements, with best practice case examples, checklists and tools. This thoroughly practical guide brings together over 25 years of the author's experience negotiating in a variety of countries and contexts to give you the confidence to negotiate any kind of contract or agreement, large or small. Using a 'solution-focused' approach which centres around preferred outcomes rather than conflicts, and on questioning and listening to the other party rather than trying to convince or impose and making assumptions, this pragmatic book will help build your profile as an ethical and respected negotiator. From contextual analysis and goal preparation to the importance of communication and building an offer, it cuts through the theory and clearly outlines the skills needed to influence the outcome and implementation of any negotiation"– Provided by publisher.
Identifiers: LCCN 2021038087 (print) | LCCN 2021038088 (ebook) | ISBN
    9781398601802 (paperback) | ISBN 9781398601826 (hardback) | ISBN 9781398601819 (ebook)
Subjects: LCSH: Negotiation–United States. | Partnership–United States. |
    BISAC: BUSINESS & ECONOMICS / Negotiating
Classification: LCC BF637.N4 D375 2021 (print) | LCC BF637.N4 (ebook) |
    DDC 158/.5–dc23
LC record available at https://lccn.loc.gov/2021038087
LC ebook record available at https://lccn.loc.gov/2021038088

Typeset by Integra Software Services, Pondicherry
Print production managed by Jellyfish
Printed and bound by CPI Group (UK) Ltd, Croydon CR0 4YY

CONTENTS

PREFACE

Why this handbook

In the end, if you want a different result, try a different approach.
(INSPIRED BY ALFRED EINSTEIN)

As a professional, I have been involved in negotiations and partnership-building in business, politics and humanitarian action for the last 25 years, using a specific methodology and approach that has proven to be highly successful. This led me to develop and run workshops on how to negotiate and how to build lasting partnerships and collaborations, in which I share the tools I have developed, the accompanying mindset and my experiences with my participants. The feedback I have received, even many years after their participation in the workshop, as well as my track record in 'real life' negotiations, has proven time and time again that this particular approach to negotiation works in a deep way, bringing about surprising partnerships and results, together with lasting collaborations. What follows originates from the repeated requests of participants for me to write a book to explain this model and its tools, with real anonymized examples, and ultimately to share the value of what they have learned with others. My customers, who come from a variety of backgrounds, be it universities, technical and engineering schools, life science research institutes, multinational companies, international organizations, non-profit organizations and small and medium enterprises (SMEs), encouraged me to start on this adventure. Their enthusiasm and trust have kept this very special project alive: to write a useful and practical handbook about how to build successful, lasting and ethical negotiations. For that I deeply thank them.

We live in an increasingly complex and connected world where stand-alone companies and 'island' projects are a thing of the past or a rarity.

We need to connect to and with others. We need to function in an inter-related and interconnected world in which we cannot easily do without the skills, services and products others have developed. We also need others in order to make, develop and sell our products and services. When we talk about interconnected systems, in which people have little choice but to work together and collaborate to live, let alone thrive, a system of managing this interconnectedness is needed. We require this in our profes-sional environments to collaborate and build partnerships, as well as in our personal and family environments. There are several ways to manage these relationships, including imposing, convincing, haggling – all of which will be discussed in the next chapter.

What this handbook will concentrate on is another approach, one that involves a totally different way of considering the other party with whom we need to engage. This route is negotiation, with its very specific characteristics.

When we are called on to negotiate, it is because we need a contract signed or an agreement reached. We need to agree on a specific result, we want to build a partnership, to manage a project, to set up a collaboration, to settle a family issue. If we are going to invest time, energy and money in negotiating, it is ultimately because we realize that alone we cannot reach our goal as successfully as we would taking the others on board: we actu-ally also need these 'others'. This approach is what differentiates this handbook from other negotiation books. It offers an approach, a five-step guide and practical tools as well as a mindset. If we spend this amount of time and energy for the agreement to backfire as soon as our backs are turned, or shortly thereafter, then we have wasted our, our company's, our family's time.

This book is based on the view that to negotiate is to get what one wants, of course, but not alone. It is instead based on achieving one's goal together with and thanks to the other party. To negotiate is to make good use of what the other party wants (their goal) to help us get closer to our aim through the dynamics of exchanging various elements. All those involved have a say in the outcome, which is fundamental in our complex environment in which we need others in order to move forward and put into place what has been decided. We must ensure their buy-in and commitment to make any agree-ment live. For all stakeholders to be committed to put into action the agreed plan or partnership, to collaborate effectively, each one needs to have their interest, their concern that is being taken into account in the (result of the) deal, in the outcome, in the agreement. Buy-in is fundamental to the sense of ownership, which in turn will lead to increased commitment – and resources – to get the job done. Building such partnerships based on an understanding of each party's needs and wishes and – wherever possible – in helping each party achieve at least part of these makes for more solid and longer-lasting agreements. This handbook walks readers through how to achieve such partnerships and sustainable collaborations.

I was trained in solution-focused coaching for individuals and organizations, and have been influenced by solution-focused approaches in most of my work. During my studies, and throughout the work I have done with different teams and individuals, I have noted many similarities between solution-focused approaches and the negotiation methodology that is described in my handbook, some of which are:

- Both are built with the end result in mind, i.e. a focus on the goal that one seeks to achieve (one's ambitious 'preferred future', or the answer to the 'miracle' question: *'If I could do what I want, what would it be?'*, *'What would the ideal partnership look like?'*).

- Both are built on hope and possibilities, goals and pathways. It is not about what one doesn't want but about what one ideally would like, and how to best get there – together with the other stakeholders. *'If I do not want this situation, what do I want instead?'*

- Both concentrate on what is needed to get to a desired state or path, i.e. the negotiation conditions and mapping the necessary 'small steps'.

- Both underline the need to be highly creative. Imagination is the key to success.

- Both require acute listening and observation skills.

- Both are *highly focused* on the other party, the people we are dealing with and talking to.

- Throughout, the focus is on what could be done, on what has already been achieved or agreed upon.

- The interest, i.e. the motivation of all involved parties, is fundamental.

Thus I feel that my negotiation model could be called a 'solution-focused negotiation' model.

In this handbook you will find practical ideas and tools that can help make your collaborations fruitful, respectful and respected. The model presented is simple, straightforward and incredibly powerful. Used, tried and tested over more than two decades, its strength comes from its simplicity and ethical approach to dealing with others. It is based on considering the other party as a partner with whom you need to build a relationship, this other who is your best opportunity, not an adversary.

The best indicator of a successful negotiation is its sustainability, in other words the lasting effect it results in: it must be productive and fair in that each party finds all or part of their interest and needs in the agreement. We all spend a great part of our life negotiating – so why not try this model, test it and see how useful it can be for you?

A final note on gender-specific terms: I use 'he' and 'she' interchangeably to ease the flow of both reading and writing. When a gender-specific term is used it should be understood as referring to all genders, with no preference.

The book is divided into five parts:

- **Part One** covers the best mindset for successful negotiations, the overall process and necessary prerequisites.

- **Part Two** explores in detail the two steps linked with the preparation – both of the context and of the goal – of a negotiation.

- **Part Three** focuses on communication and meeting the other party. This third step – the encounter – is discussed, along with some issues pertaining to online negotiations. A negotiator–communicator toolbox is presented, together with some insights on social intuition and its importance in managing effectively social relationships and the encounters. Cognitive elements such as emotion management and posture are also covered.

- **Part Four** talks about the final two steps: the offer and the implementation.

- **Part Five** brings some thought and considerations to gender, and the potential influence of gender on negotiation encounters and outcome.

Finally, in the appendix are some real simplified and anonymized examples of the various steps in practice.

ACKNOWLEDGEMENTS

The fabric of this book is woven from all the encounters, the books and research, the participants I have trained with their stories and examples, the individuals and companies for whom I have negotiated, and finally the very special friends who have offered me constant encouragement.

I am deeply grateful for all who enabled this approach to be written about.

I would like to offer very special thanks and tremendous gratitude to Danièle Castle, whose advice, skills, trust and enthusiasm have proven invaluable. Danièle was my sparring partner throughout this endeavour. Without her precious help and encouragement I am not sure you would be holding this handbook today.

I would also like to thank Guy de Brett for his patient help in improving my English and for his encouragement throughout, and Pascale Dethurens for designing the puzzle graphics that so accurately depict the process.

My deep thanks to Kogan Page and their team without whom this book would not exist, and to Amy Minshull for having believed in me and my project; her quiet presence meant a lot.

And finally thank you to all my participants, customers, partners in negotiations – whose interest, engagement and feedback over the years encouraged me to embark on this adventure.

Mindset, process and prerequisites

Part One covers the best mindset for successful negotiations as well as the overall process, its five steps and necessary prerequisites.

01

Introduction and mindset

What is negotiation? What makes a good and respected negotiator? How do you define a successful negotiation?

When faced with a situation in which you need someone to help you get what you want, when you want or have to bring people together to collaborate, when a conflict needs to be managed, any time you require others to achieve the desired result, there are several strategies you can use. This chapter explores different ways of handling such situations, moving from unilateral approaches to a more bilateral or multilateral approach. The advantages and disadvantages of each strategy will be pointed out through examples, with a special focus on the one bilateral approach – negotiation.

Why do people tend to resist unilateral approaches? How should the other party be viewed in a bilateral approach? Why do people engage more when they have been listened to and taken into consideration? This chapter will explore somes answers to these questions.

The mindset with which the other party is considered is extremely impor-tant. This mindset follows the similar underlying premise as Nelson Mandela did, when he pointed out during his life-long struggle that if you want to make peace with your enemy, you need to work with your enemy. Then they become your partner,[1] someone with whom you can work. This negotiation approach views your counterpart as your opportunity. This very specific mindset is linked to being an excellent and respected negotiator and will be explained. Realizing that your counterpart is your best opportunity (partner) for reaching a deal will have noticeable effects both on how the encounters take place and on negotiated outcomes.

Working with the other party

The most important indicator of a good negotiation is its lasting result. Negotiation is often viewed as a struggle, a metaphorical wrestling match that involves scoring points, winning, 'good guy/bad guy' tactics, struggling, manipulating, even damaging the other, at times to the detriment of the relationship. These tactics endanger any long-term collaboration or partnership. What if there were another way to approach negotiation? A solution-focused approach? An opportunity-based approach? A more positive, respectful and enjoyable approach? What if negotiating was something which you could actually look forward to?

Negotiation is an art, the art of exploring how each party can get what they want, where each party explores *the conditions under which they could say yes* to the other party's requests and needs, while ensuring that their own needs are met.

The world abounds with examples of – at times spectacular – negotiations that have failed, peace agreements that have never been put into effect, business deals that have never actually happened. Consider a change of paradigm. How would it feel if you had the certainty that you needed the other party to achieve your aim, an aim that was *better* reached together than alone? If you considered them as partners?

If you knew deep inside yourself that the key to success lay with working *with* the other rather than *against* that person, your whole attitude would change.

Imagine negotiation as:

- a process, a discussion and a collaboration – not a struggle or a battle
- enhancing each stakeholder's goals, thus enabling each party to grow
- a clear, simple and realistic way of managing relationships in a transparent and respectful way

Different strategies for handling a conflict of interest

Let's work through an example illustrating most common behaviours when faced with conflicting interests, and where you need a person or a group to obtain something.

EXAMPLE

Imagine the following situation: a last-minute board meeting has been organized this evening to handle some critical problems linked to a very important project of which you are project manager. Your presence is required by the main sponsor of the project. This situation is incredibly difficult for you, as this evening you have organized a special surprise party for your daughter's 18th birthday, which is a significant event. Friends and extended family are coming over. It is also important for you not only as helper and organizer, but also simply for your presence: you have been working away from home a lot recently and have promised your daughter that you will be there for her birthday.

You have made up your mind. Even if your work is important, you have decided that you wish to go to your daughter's party, without jeopardizing the project advancement that will be discussed tonight with the project board and sponsor.

What can you do?

When you want something that involves other people, or when there is a conflict of interest, one or several courses of action tend to be used, almost automatically, amongst which can be identified attempts to:

- convince
- impose
- threaten
- buy
- manipulate
- haggle and compromise
- arbitrate
- suggest solutions and alternatives
- give up

Convince

To convince someone is to 'make somebody believe that something is true', and comes from the Latin word *convincere*, from *con* (with) and *vincer* (conquer), so to overcome or defeat in argument. You use arguments that are solid and meaningful *to you* in order to convince the other to change their mind, to think like you do. Without necessarily realizing it, you are trying to influence them to '*stop being them*', i.e. different from you, so as to *become like you.*

When you convince someone, you put forward what is important to you and what has a value for you; you bring in your arguments. You seek to influence the other so that what is important to you becomes important to them.

How do most people react when faced with, for instance, a seller trying to convince them that their product or service is the best and that they really should buy it? The more the seller tries to argue their point, insist and sell, the more people have a tendency to turn away, to refuse the purchase, to block. This is often in reaction to feeling coerced or harassed rather than from lack of interest in the product being sold. Most people resent being told how they should feel and what they should do, particularly when faced with convincing reasons *that do not come from them.*[2]

EXAMPLE OF CONVINCING

'Thank you for having organized the meeting, but tonight is not possible. You have a family too, I know you can understand. You know how important my children are to me, and my daughter is 18 today. Please try to understand my situation, my daughter would be so upset, even angry if I didn't show up. I am sure you realize how upsetting it would be for me and my family. It would make my life on the project much easier if I were to show my family that I can work hard and at the same time be present for important moments such as birthdays...'

Impose

To impose something (on somebody) is to decide and simply tell the other person about your decision, to force somebody to have to deal with something that is difficult or unpleasant. '*This is how it should be.*' In this strategy you take a unilateral decision and impose it on the other party, regardless of what they may say or think. Have you ever had a decision imposed on you? How did you like it? More importantly, how did you react?

EXAMPLE OF IMPOSING

'Thank you for the invitation but I will not be attending the meeting this evening.'

Threaten

To threaten is to muscle in on the other: '*If you don't do this* (i.e. if you don't say yes) *this will happen.*' In other words, if you do not get your own way, these are the possible negative consequences that will occur.

EXAMPLE OF THREATENING

'If I don't go to my daughter's party this evening my family will be really upset and this could have effects on my work and productivity...'

Buy

To buy the other person's agreement or acceptance is done by putting a price on their 'yes' ('*If you say yes, this is what you will get in exchange*'). In extreme situations this can be compared to corruption.

EXAMPLE OF BUYING

'If you let me attend my daughter's party this evening, I will be able to come in to work this weekend and I will be able to count on my family's support during the rest of the project.'

Manipulate

To manipulate can equate to trying to control the other or to get them to change without them realizing it, with an intention that is hidden and probably negative; if it wasn't negative you would speak your arguments out loud which would thus become 'convincing'. Often, in situations where manipulation is strong, it is because the person manipulating does not think the other party will agree if the goal is clear.

EXAMPLE OF MANIPULATING

'You may have heard through your partner that I have my daughter's birthday party this evening. If I am not at home this evening, I am afraid my partner will be so upset. And you know what they are like. I cannot imagine what they might say the next time they see your spouse.'

Haggle and compromise

To haggle or make a compromise means you give a little and they give a little: 'an agreement made between two people or groups in which each side gives up some of the things they want'. This is the one course of action in which everyone gets something, but no one gets what they want. Each party tends to leave the table with, in their mind, what they have lost and not what they have gained. Compromise essentially means dividing something, assuming that something is divisible, leaving nobody satisfied… and is usually not a creative outcome.[3]

Although at times compromises can be life-saving or the only way forward – e.g. in some political conflicts and divorce situations – the downsides are high, with the risk that frustration stops the compromised result being put into practice. Norwegian sociologist and principal founder of the discipline of peace and conflict studies, Johan Vincent Galtung, notes that often, contrary to popular belief, compromise is a consensus about an outcome that satisfies nobody, with the conflict still present but not exploding because the contradictions have become less acute.[4]

EXAMPLE OF COMPROMISING AND HAGGLING

'How about I come to the board meeting from 18:30 to 20:00 and then leave? No?… OK then, I could leave at 20:30…' (in this case most likely leaving boss, daughter and self frustrated).

Arbitrate

Arbitration, put very simply, is the process of settling an argument or a disagreement by somebody who is not involved. Strictly speaking, an arbitrator is a neutral third party to whom the power of decision has been delegated. The arbitrator usually needs to decide between two options/parties, each having 50 per cent probability of winning.

If, however, you ask the person who is directly involved in the issue at hand, i.e. who is not neutral, to be the arbitrator, then the probability of you getting what you want falls drastically. This tactic – asking the other '*What do you think? What should I do?*' is often used to make one feel less guilty, and often follows some convincing positive statements, making the other believe they have something to say on a decision that you have already taken.

There are three possible results:

1 If the other party gives the answer you want them to answer, then all is fine, even though this may create a certain amount of frustration for them, which will need to be checked.

2 If they do not give the answer you want and you respect their decision, then it is true arbitration, and in effect you have allowed the other person to decide for you.

3 If, however, they do not give the answer you wish and you do not accept their decision, then this is not arbitration but a manipulative tactic, and you risk causing a high level of frustration as you are giving the other party a false sense of power. E.g. '*I am asking you to make a decision that I have in fact already made*' (see example).

Have you ever been asked for your opinion and had it ignored? If so, how did you feel? And how did you respond the next time the same person asked you for your opinion?

EXAMPLE OF ARBITRATION

'I am stuck – I am delighted that you have gone to such lengths to organize this board meeting this evening, but I have my daughter's 18th birthday party, which is also really important to me. So, on the one hand I have my project and this meeting, and on the other my family duty and daughter's birthday party. What should I do? What do you think?'

Suggest solutions and alternatives

When faced with a problematic situation, you think of various potential solutions or alternatives, which you then suggest to the other party. '*I have a problem, I find a solution.*' The solution you suggest is usually the one most suited to you and to your issue/problem, and you hope that the other party will agree. If they don't, the tendency is to enter into a spiral of solutions, whereby you keep bringing in new ideas, hoping that at some point one will work out and that the other will change their planning or idea to suit yours. Once again this can work, but it can also make the other party feel they have nothing to say except yes.

EXAMPLE OF SOLUTIONS

'I have an issue for this evening. Could we postpone the board meeting to tomorrow morning? Or could I send my colleague to come and represent me?'

Give up

By giving up, you let the other party have it their way and you give in. Although this can happen in sincere good faith, beware of the risk of the '*after all I have done for you*' syndrome, which can create resentfulness and accountability ('*You owe me*') in the longer term and make the other person feel guilty.

EXAMPLE OF GIVING UP

'Ok, I'll come to the meeting' (and give up on my daughter's birthday party).

All these strategies work. They all have consequences. And they all share three characteristics:

1 They are unilateral, i.e. they only consider one point of view – your own. Any unilateral approach is based on one party only and sends out the message to the other that what really is important is what you want and what is important to you, not to them. That your opinion, needs, desires are what matter. A person faced with such behaviour usually feels ignored and unimportant and has two main ways of reacting: either non-existent, i.e.

they give in and say yes; or existent, i.e. they resist and say no or hinder the outcome or relationship.

2 They – consciously or not – consider that the other party is *the problem*. In other words, if your boss hadn't called the meeting this evening, you would be in a good mood and looking forward to your daughter's party. If the party had been scheduled for this weekend rather than for this evening, then all would be well with the world and you wouldn't worry about going to the meeting. *It is because of the other person that you cannot do what you want to do* without possible negative consequences, and this is why you try to convince them to change, impose your viewpoint, try to buy their agreement, even possibly manipulate to get your own way.

3 In order to get what you want, you need the other party. You actually need your boss to be able to get what you want, which is to go to your daughter's birthday party *without negative consequences* for your project. As soon as you realize you need the other person, they become an opportunity, in fact in this precise moment *your best opportunity*. And when this happens, the process becomes bilateral, or, if there are many stakeholders, multilateral. You enter into a real interaction, where the interests of all parties need to be *understood and taken into account*, and this is called negotiation.

1.1

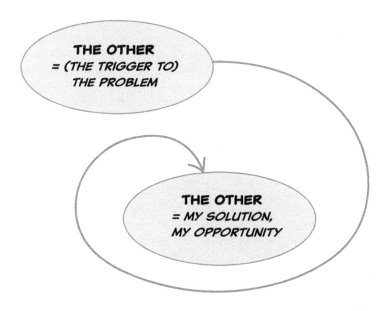

Negotiation

EXAMPLE OF NEGOTIATION

'My daughter is turning 18 today and I have organized a special party for her which I really would like to attend. What can I do so that my absence this evening is not damaging to the project?'

Negotiation happens when each party has the space to engage in the process. *Negotiation is based on finding out the conditions under which you can get what you want.* Although not a magic wand, it is the only way to ensure all parties' wishes and needs are taken into account. The difference between negotiation and arbitration is that you are not asking the other to make a decision, but you are asking them *what needs to be done* for them to say yes.

In the above example, the boss might answer '*No problem, send a colleague to the meeting*', or '*Let's meet now to prepare your part of the meeting so I can explain your solutions and ideas*'. Or they might say, '*Sorry, not possible, you have to be present*' in which case you will need to try another more unilateral approach.

Negotiation is a choice, one amongst many ways of handling certain situations and interactions. It is the choice of engaging the other party in the process. At times you might choose to convince, for instance when lobbying; you might need to impose, as you would if you were putting into place security standards; or you might have to offer a specific solution, such as an IT engineer who needs to fix a bug would be expected to do. However, whenever a good working relationship is needed to put an agreement into action, try negotiation first. It is the one way to ensure long lasting results and collaboration, because it takes into account each party's needs, wishes and views, and is more respectful, trying to *do with* rather than *against*.

If the answer is no, if your attempt to find a negotiated agreement has failed, then you can revert to any one of the strategies outlined above, taking into account that each one will have its own consequences.

The way you consider and treat someone has a strong influence on the way they will treat you in return.[5] It is in your best interest to treat the

I want to go to my daughter's party with no professional problem   1.2

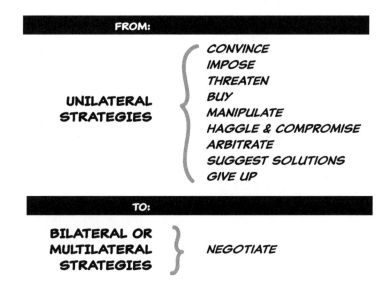

FROM:

UNILATERAL
STRATEGIES

CONVINCE
IMPOSE
THREATEN
BUY
MANIPULATE
HAGGLE & COMPROMISE
ARBITRATE
SUGGEST SOLUTIONS
GIVE UP

TO:

BILATERAL OR
MULTILATERAL
STRATEGIES

NEGOTIATE

other party as a partner and an opportunity, not as a problem or a hindrance. For many reasons, you should know they are your best opportunity to get what you want. Whatever the issue at hand, if you are engaged in talking with them it is because you need them. Being conscious of this will influence your behaviour, posture, attitude and communication style, which in turn will affect how the other responds. As Nelson Mandela stated, you tend to attract integrity and honour if that is how you regard those with whom you are.[6]

Negotiation can thus be compared to building a puzzle *together* rather than playing a chess game *against*. It is a bilateral or multilateral way of getting what one wants, not *regardless* of the other party, but *with* them. Exploring together in detail the issues and conditions of all parties should enable each party to get closer to what they want through the dynamics of exchange, because you will be trying to give the other what they want *under your conditions*. If you constantly keep in your mind that the other party is an opportunity, and their wants and needs a positive energy, this new state of mind will fundamentally influence the way the negotiation will take place, as well as its resulting agreement being put into practice or enforced.

Chapter 1: summary points

- Negotiation is about getting what you want *under certain conditions*. It is about engaging in a bilateral process that takes into account the various parties needed or involved in putting the agreement into place. It is about collective creativity and partnership-building.

- The other party always represents an opportunity as a partner in negotiation. This is because you need them in order to reach an agreement that is going to require their engagement and commitment to be respected.

- Each party must be taken into account throughout the process, with their specific needs and concerns.

- A successful negotiation is one in which a lasting agreement is reached and put into place. In other words, the main criterion for judging the success of a negotiation is whether what has been negotiated is actually respected.

Notes

1 Nelson Mandela, quoted by OSCE Chairperson-in-Office, Deputy Prime Minister and Minister for Foreign Affairs and Trade, Eamon Gilmore, 27 April 2012

2 'Whether you are dealing with an animal or a child, to convince is to weaken.' Colette (1941) *Le Pur et l'Impur*, Aux Armes de France

3 'Compromise is the comfort of the poor, he who knows so little about what can come out of a conflict that he believes compromise is the only alternative. Compromise is often a consensus about an outcome that satisfies nobody... the conflict is still there glowing if not exploding because the contradictions have become less acute.' J Galtung (2000) *Conflict Transformation by Peaceful Means: Participants' Manual*, United Nations Disaster Management Training Programme. www.transcend.org/pctrcluj2004/TRANSCEND_manual.pdf (archived at https://perma.cc/NAR5-55DG)

4 J Galtung (2000) *Conflict Transformation by Peaceful Means: Participants' Manual*, United Nations Disaster Management Training Programme. www. transcend.org/pctrcluj2004/TRANSCEND_manual.pdf (archived at https:// perma.cc/NAR5-55DG)

5 E Fehr and S Gächter. Fairness and retaliation: The economics of reciprocity, *Journal of Economic Perspectives*, 2000, 14 (3), 159–82. 'In social psychology, reciprocity is a social norm of responding to a positive action with another positive action, rewarding kind actions. As a social construct, reciprocity means that in response to friendly actions, people are frequently much nicer and much more cooperative than predicted by the self-interest model; conversely, in response to hostile actions they are frequently much more nasty and even brutal.'

6 N Mandela (2010) *Conversation With Myself*, Macmillan, New York

02

The five-step process

Characteristics and focus

This chapter outlines the five steps that make up the negotiation process. Breaking down the process in such a systematic way will help structure the negotiation and give the negotiator practical insight on how to proceed with a clear methodology and specific tools.

The characteristics of a negotiation will start to be explored in this chapter and will be continued in Chapter 3. When called on to negotiate, your focus of primary attention changes depending on which step you are engaged in. First of all, where to focus – whether on yourself or on the other party – will be covered. By way of an example, we show why knee-jerk reactions should be avoided, and, when faced with a sudden request or suggestion, what the most appropriate way to react is. The fact that negotiation is and should be an iterative process is the next topic. You will find out why successful negotiations often go through several rounds, necessitating careful planning and at times a good deal of patience.

The five steps and their focus

Negotiation is a process that takes place in different stages, each with a different focus. The methodology in this handbook identifies the following five steps:

Step 1: contextual analysis

Step 2: goal analysis

Step 3: encounters – being face-to-face

Step 4: offer

Step 5: implementation

2.1

These five steps are explained in detail in Chapters 4 through to 11. Followed one by one, they create a constructive negotiation process. In order to carry out these five steps successfully, there are certain prerequisites that you will need to adopt in terms of focus and how you approach the negotiation. These are relevant to the negotiation steps 2 to 4, and will be described below.

Where to focus and on what?

Step	Prerequisites and focus
Step 1: contextual analysis	Focus on facts and on self
Step 2: goal analysis	Focus on self – stay in your ego bubble
Step 3: encounter	Focus on the other party
Step 4: offer	Focus on self through the other's viewpoint and reactions
Step 5: implementation	Focus on self through the other's viewpoint and reactions

MAIN FOCUS   THE FIVE STEPS   2.2

1 CONTEXTUAL ANALYSIS

2 GOAL ANALYSIS
Know what I want

3 ENCOUNTER(S)
Know what the other wants

4 OFFER
Exchange

5 IMPLEMENTATION

During goal analysis: focus on self in 'ego bubble'

In the goal analysis (step 2, see Chapter 5), when you are working on your goal, you need to lock yourself in an '**ego bubble**'. This requires you to be totally focused on yourself, you or your issue: your project, your organization, your customer, your family… There must be no room for any thought of the other party and what they might want. This is because as soon as you think of the other party, you will tend to downgrade what you want (self-talk, convincing yourself '*They will never say yes, they will not agree*', '*This is not possible*', etc).

Empathy, both cognitive and emotional, is to be avoided at all costs at this stage. An incredibly common and strong assumption most people have is that '*The other person will not let me get what I want. They are in there to block or annoy me.*' It is therefore of utmost importance to block out any thought of the other party in your preparation and to concentrate solely on you and your goal, using a powerful tool, the roadmap, which will be explained in Chapter 5.

In fact, throughout this entire process, your starting point is always yourself. Your preparation is all about you and the best situation you wish to achieve. The starting point could be '*If I had a magic wand…*', or '*If I could do what I wanted…*'.

During encounters: focus on the other

In the encounters (step 3, Chapter 6), when you are face to face with the other party, whether through direct or virtual communication, you need to be totally focused on '**the other**', i.e. the other party. During the encounters, you are no longer centred on yourself like you were during the preparation; you are now fully concentrated on the other party, on what they want, what is important for them, what has a value for them, their issues, their concerns, their fears. The fact that you were first centred on yourself makes it much easier to then focus on your counterpart because you are safe in your knowledge of what you want, and therefore you will tend to be less or not at all influenced by them. You approach them from a safe spot – yourself. Furthermore, if you think of yourself first and only then of the other party, it will be much easier to see them as an opportunity, as an *enabler*.

During the offer: focus back on self but now through the other's eyes

When you are building your offer (step 4, Chapter 10), you come back to yourself again, but this time '*through the other party's eyes*', i.e. you focus on your goal, but this time based on how the other party reacted to what you want and said (did they say *yes*, *no*, *maybe…*?).

Avoiding knee-jerk reactions

Automatic reactions of responding and taking position with *yes*, *no* or *maybe* when someone asks you something should be avoided at all cost. You do not want to give an answer you might regret, or fail to ask for something in exchange for you agreeing with what the other person wants or suggests.

What this solution-focused model of negotiation puts forward is first the acknowledgement of a request ('*I take note of what you are suggesting, and will come back to you, thank you*') and postponement of a direct reaction or quick response. You then need to *go up one level*, into your 'ego bubble', and ask yourself: what do *you* want out of this request or offer, how can *you* turn it into an opportunity? Do *you* really want this to happen? And if so, *under what conditions*?

In other words, anchoring yourself in your 'ego bubble' will make sure you think carefully before accepting or committing to anything. It ensures that you do not automatically say no or yes, and requires you to think of a set of conditions that would get you closer to a good deal for yourself. By not reacting directly, you actually enhance the possibility of deciding to accept the offer *under certain conditions*.

EXAMPLE

You are a team leader and Tina, the software developer working in your team, comes to ask you if she can do a specific project management course.

Knee jerk answer: you either accept or refuse her request, having studied the course information.

Acknowledgement answer: *'I will think about your request and come back to you latest end next week with my answer'*.

Ego bubble goal analysis:

1 Do I actually want someone in my team to do a project management course?

2 If yes, do I want this to be a certifiable course with a recognized exam?

3 Which particular project management methodology would *I* like for my team/the company?

4 Would this project management methodology be useful to others in the team?

5 Do I want a presentation to the team to be made?

6 Do I want Tina to do this course or do I think Frank would be most suited to it?

7 Do I have a project coming up for which Tina could be project manager?

8 By when do I want Tina to have finished the course? And completed her certificate?

9 Do I want Tina to make sure that her work is done even if on a course, ie to work overtime if necessary?

10 …

The fact that you come back into your ego bubble for this reflection will enable you to talk to your colleague in a different manner, thus changing the dynamics of the discussion. Rather than simply agreeing or refusing her request, you now *aim to give her what she wants under your conditions*. In other words, you assess what would make it worthwhile for you to say yes.

When you next meet your employee, your answer could be:

'*Yes you can go to do this project management course* (your colleague gets what she wants) *and* (for it to be worthwhile for me and the team) *I would like you to prepare a management summary for your colleagues. I would also like you take on project X which is starting in six months' time. Finally, I would like you to make a comparative study of the various project management methods used in our company.*'

These are the conditions for you to say '*Yes*'.

It is always beneficial to ask yourself under what conditions you would say yes. What would it take for you to agree to her request? In other words, a negotiator should avoid a straight yes or no, but should always first *seek to find out the conditions under which they will say yes*. Saying yes straight away

2.3

EXAMPLE:
YOU RECEIVE A REQUEST

1 *The trigger is a request made by someone. Rather than reacting directly...*

2 *... acknowledge the request,* GO UP ONE LEVEL *into your ego bubble and ask yourself what it would take for you to consider saying yes*

3 *Then give your conditional acceptance (or not)*

often creates a sense of 'I owe you', whereas exchanging conditions makes for a more balanced deal. Look out for the opportunity in any situation!

Negotiation is an iterative process

Negotiation is not a linear process: it is highly improbable – and rarely advisable – that you would enter a meeting, listen, question, understand, build an offer and sign an agreement in one single sitting. Even when you're well prepared, a negotiation that is the slightest bit complex will raise new information, unforeseen issues and tactics that you did not anticipate.[1]

Negotiation is an iterative process whereby rounds of negotiation are often the norm, particularly in the political, economic and trade fields. Negotiation requires repeated interactions. For example, by October 2019 the USA and China were planning their 13th round of trade negotiations, which started in 2018.[2]

First, you carefully prepare what you want (your goal), then you have one or several encounters during which you will most certainly add elements (conditions) and learn relevant information. After several encounters, once you have received and given all the information needed, then and *only then* are you in a position to make a first offer, which will in turn be discussed and improved upon. Patience is a highly useful attitude to have when negotiating. For instance, being patient means there is less risk that you will commit too fast or get (over) excited; patience gives you and the other party time to think, and builds space in which you might find out certain elements or new information. Pressing for a result can be interpreted as eagerness to close the deal, and can lead to increased stakes.

The fact that the process is iterative lowers the pressure of an immediate or quick result: when you are face-to-face with your counterpart (during the encounter step), no commitments are made; you are in a mode of sharing information. The fact that you are not pushing or putting the other party under pressure will have an influence on how you behave and communicate, on your choice of words and your attitude, and therefore on how they respond. Trust is best built over time, through formal and informal meetings and discussions. It is worth remembering that your own attitude, posture and communication style have a great influence on how fruitful a meeting will be. The encounters will tend to be less challenging, less awe-inspiring and the tone more creative, flexible and open. See more on that in the encounter step (see Chapter 6).

2.4

AN ITERATIVE PROCESS

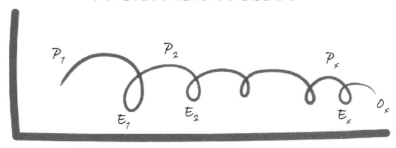

DURATION

1   Prepare for first roadmap
2   Have first encounter.
3   Add to roadmap.
4   Have second encounter.
5   Make first offer and discuss.
6   Make the second offer possible.
7   And so on until the deal is clinched.

Chapter 2: summary points

- Negotiation is a five-step process. Each step is distinct with its own focus and tool. The overall mindset remains the same throughout: the other is your opportunity and is to be considered as such.

- Negotiation is an iterative process. This means that patience will be necessary and sufficient time will need to be planned. It is always advisable to plan your negotiations, allowing sufficient time for several rounds of encounters. Patience sends strong signals.

- At each and every step of the process, different areas of focus are to be maintained. During the preparation step (goal analysis), the focus is on your own goal and you lock yourself in your 'ego bubble'.

- Whilst in the encounter step, your focus is on the other party and on finding out what they want.

- When engaged in the offer step, the focus is back on yourself, but this time taking into account what the other party wants and how they reacted to your needs and requests.

Notes

1 M Bazerman and D Malhotra. It's not intuitive: Strategies for negotiating more rationally, *Negotiation*, May 2006

2 RTS news. www.rts.ch/info. Reuters. www.reuters.com/article/us-usa-trade-china-talk-explainer/u-s-china-trade-talks-where-they-are-and-whats-at-stake-idUSKCN1TT2JF (archived at https://perma.cc/Q6NX-9V74)

03

Prerequisites and positioning your goal (linkage tool)

For a negotiation to take place, several conditions need to be present. It is not enough for one party simply to decide they want to negotiate. This chapter first explores the four prerequisites for a negotiation to take place and the importance of 'interest'. Interest is key to the lasting success of the negotiated agreement or partnership, even if the interest differs from party to party. In other words, without interest there will be no lasting negotiated agreement.

We then look at the linkage tool. This tool is used to position one's goal, to clarify what is negotiable and what is non-negotiable, to understand one's motivation (both intrinsic and extrinsic) and to decide on one's real opening point – the point beyond which you give space to the other party and start to negotiate. Clarity and understanding will help you structure your thoughts and give you a stronger foundation from which to move towards the other in the right mindset.

We follow that with a discussion of motivation and the relationship between motivation, resilience and confidence, when negotiating will be explored. The way you set your goal plays a fundamental role in predicting your success in reaching it. Why is it so important to choose an inspiring and positively stated goal? Some of the reasons will be suggested, including the fact that there seems to be a definite connection between goal-setting and parts of the brain.

Prerequisites

There are four prerequisites for a negotiation process to be able to take place.

1 *Volition:*   Your first prerequisite is the volition to negotiate. You need to *want* to negotiate. Negotiation is a choice, which may not be suitable for all situations. At times you may wish to impose (specific behaviours at home like brushing teeth, or security measures in a factory, objectives for a team…), convince (lobbying for a nature conservation project, a political issue…), or suggest a solution (to an IT problem…) – see Chapter 1.

2 *Opportunity (i.e. possibility):*   The second prerequisite is that your wish to negotiate must correspond to the readiness of the other party to engage in the process. There needs to be a willingness from the other side. It may take time helping them find out what their interest could be and discover what could be the positive outcome for them if they have not thought of it. If, however, you are faced with someone who really does not want to negotiate, there is nothing you can do. In this case it could be advisable to postpone to a later date when (if) circumstances have changed and may be more promising.

THE FOUR PREREQUISITES   *3.1*
FOR A NEGOTIATION TO BE ABLE TO TAKE PLACE

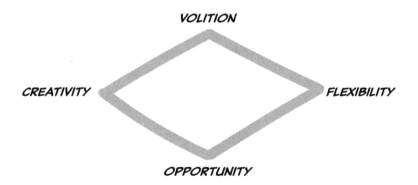

3 *Creativity:* The third prerequisite is the capacity to invent what doesn't exist, to think of new or different options, to imagine conditions, to create and enable a capacity for exchange, to be open to possible new solutions and ideas.

4 *Flexibility:* Together with creativity, you need flexibility. One cannot go without the other. It is only through being flexible that you will get something through the process of exchange. *You are willing to move away from A in exchange for B.* Without flexibility there is no possibility for exchange. Furthermore, inflexibility breeds blocking attitudes and intransigence, thereby hindering the entire process.

Finally, of paramount importance and what keeps both parties in the negotiation is **interest**. And this focus on interest remains throughout the entire five steps.

The parties involved *do not need to share the same interest*; however, each party needs to have their own interest taken into account, implicitly or explicitly, at some point. Unfortunately there is often a tendency to expect and want the other party to share one's interest, which leads one to start arguing and convincing.

3.2
THE CEMENT THAT HOLDS
THE ENTIRE PROCESS TOGETHER

EXAMPLE

Let us imagine you are involved in a project to distribute and install dustbins in all public parks in a major town. When you meet the town officials, it would be a lot easier for you if they were already aware of the littering issue and interested in your project to help tidy up the town. You could then concentrate on getting started. If, however, they are not aware of or interested in either littering or tidying up, the tendency would be for you to start arguing your case, trying to find convincing arguments and justifying them, rather than discussing the conditions under which they would be willing to support the project.

The danger with this is that all parties can lose sight of the end result, because they get lost in a debate about what is most important to one or to the other. One cannot negotiate an opinion or a value; these tend to be highly personal. In other words, seeking to convince the other party that your interest is more important can backfire as you start discussing (at best) or arguing about (at worst) the reasons why you may want or need something.

You need to spend your energy trying to find out what their interest is or at least making sure that it is taken into account, even if not clearly stated. In the example above, this might be a worry about the proliferation of rats, that the town has a small budget for cleaning, that the image of litter is not attractive to tourism...

If you are faced with someone who either does not know what they want or who is unclear about it, it will take more time and finer communication skills to (help them) find out. And if you are faced with someone who really has no interest in you and in what you want to discuss, do not waste your time – it is not that you are a bad negotiator; it is simply that there is no interest in proceeding. In this case you might want to work on finding out and giving more information (see Chapter 4).

> EXAMPLE
>
> Fred works in a nature conservation non-governmental organization and is fundraising for a large project to set up a nature conservation reserve and save endangered species. Fred contacts a large multinational company for funds. Their main interests are to have the right to tax exemption, to build a good image and promote marketing material. The actual project topic is of little or no importance to them. If Fred spends his time trying to convince them of the importance of protecting this endangered species, he may well lose the opportunity of listening to their needs, of finding out what is most important to them and what they want in order to get financially involved and build the partnership (e.g. *'You fund us, we let you use our image in your annual report and get a tax benefit for giving to charity'*).

Parties do not need to have the same interest for the deal to happen, but **interest is key to the success** of the process and needs to be present from start to end, for the negotiated agreement to actually be respected and put into place. Often in later stages of a negotiation process, if the importance of interest is downplayed there is a definite risk the parties will pull out, or fail to commit to the action plan with much energy.

The importance of preparation and being clear on your goal

Without a clear goal in negotiation, there is nothing to aim for. The biggest mistake individuals often make when going to negotiate is not being crystal clear on what they want. Why is this so important? And how do you prepare?

In the Chicago Booth Review article 'What happened to your goals?', findings from behavioural science suggest that people do better if they conceptualize goals more effectively.[1] In her article 'The science and psychology of goal-setting 101', Madhuleena Roy Chowdhury points out that neurologists working on the science of goal-setting have proved that the brain cannot distinguish between reality and imagined reality. So when you give ourselves a picture of the goal you want to achieve, when you clearly visualize it, your mind starts believing it to be real.[2] And eventually your brain begins driving you to take actions and to be more creative.

At this point it is necessary to have a clear picture of what you (think you) want, to position it in a wider context, to determine *why* you want what you want and to think about what is negotiable and what is not. For this, the linkage tool below can be very useful. You start from a general goal/idea of what you want before you fine-tune and detail it in more precise terms.

'Goals need to be self-imposed and optimistic, so people can motivate themselves... They might not meet the target, but the optimistic target is nonetheless more motivating than a pessimistic target'.[3] Chapter 5 will take you through the rules of defining a goal, including the fact that it should not be a negatively stated goal ('*I don't want...*'). Goal-setting is an essential tool for motivation and drive. Research has established a strong connection between goal-setting and success.[4] Deciding what it is you want to achieve is often a real challenge, and one that is regularly overlooked, and yet it is fundamental and will influence the entire negotiation process and outcome. The tool explained in the next section will give you some perspective on how to structure your thoughts on the topics of goal, motivation and strategies.

Preparing the what and the why: using the linkage tool to help define your goal

Once you have defined what you want to achieve in a general way, you need to reflect further on *how to position your goal*. For this, you use the linkage tool (Figure 3.3).

The linkage tool serves to help you clarify your stance for yourself. You do not share this tool with the other party.

How to use the linkage tool

First, write *what you want to achieve*, your goal, your direction, in the middle of the funnel. *This is non-negotiable:* you never negotiate what you want, you negotiate the conditions under which you can obtain it.

Next ask yourself *why you want what you want*, which you write in the top funnel shape. This represents your values, what is important to you, your motivations, your reasons why you want to achieve what you want, however personal they may be. The reason it is a funnel shape is that is gets wider and wider as your motivations get more and more personal and numerous. Be as honest and exhaustive as possible.

In some situations, your objective may have been set by your organization, by your boss, by your committee, i.e. by others. In this case it is also important for you to make sense of the objective, to find/turn it into an opportunity for yourself, so that your commitment, resilience and creativity will be enhanced, leading to a higher probability of you being successful. Your motivations (i.e. the 'why') will not necessarily be shared with the other party, to avoid getting into a process of convincing: what is important and meaningful for you may not be important and meaningful for them. Talking about your motivations increases the risk that the discussion develops into an opinion debate, which can take a lot of time and lead you away from the actual aim of the negotiation. To be successfully connected to your desired outcome you need to understand clearly the 'what' and the 'why'. The more reasons you find for wanting to achieve your goal, the more likely the goal will be achieved. Motivation breeds resilience and success. Your reasons *why* are *non-negotiable*, they are personal and belong to you.

Finally, you ask yourself *how* you could achieve your aim, which you write in the lower triangle, the upside down funnel. The *how* represents a

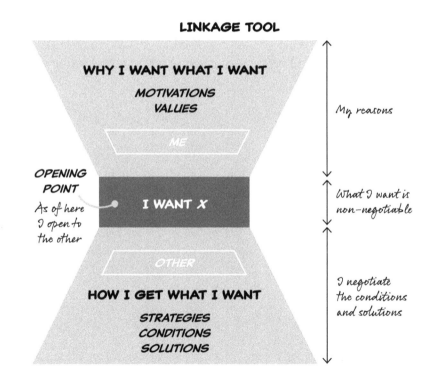

3.3   **LINKAGE TOOL**

WHY I WANT WHAT I WANT

MOTIVATIONS
VALUES

My reasons

ME

OPENING
POINT

*As of here
I open to
the other*

I WANT X

*What I want is
non-negotiable*

OTHER

HOW I GET WHAT I WANT

STRATEGIES
CONDITIONS
SOLUTIONS

*I negotiate
the conditions
and solutions*

selection of possible solutions, conditions or strategies for achieving what you want. Remember that in negotiation the *how* is co-created with the other party. Your ideas on possible means and solutions are thus negotiable, to be discussed with your counterpart, and will include their ideas. The lower part of the funnel gets wider and wider as possible solutions are never-ending. *These strategies and conditions are negotiable.*

A few words on motivation

The more you can think of what motivates you with this goal, the more committed and resilient you will be. Clarity on motivation and belief in it will in turn influence your behaviour, body language, posture and communication style.

Some of the questions you can ask yourself (particularly if your goal has been set by someone else) are:

- What is the reason behind this goal?
- What value, benefits and opportunities does it or could it bring?
- What likely impact will it have on you and on others?
- How will your life change/be improved when it is reached?

There is a difference between intrinsic motivation – doing something for the sake of it – and extrinsic motivation – doing something for the external reward. Being clear on the reasons why you want to achieve a specific goal is going to have an influence on how successful you will be in reaching it. The article 'What happened to your goals?' talks about research carried out on goal-setting, motivation and success by Fishbach and Woolley. Their findings suggest that the power of intrinsic motivation should be harnessed, as it can be a very powerful predictor of future success.[5] Therefore any element that motivates your choice of goal is important to be aware of and acknowledge.

George Wilson's study on value-centred approach to goal-setting and action planning showed that, when goal-setting, the fact that you focus on core values increases the likelihood of achieving success. Values thus have a high motivational influence.[6]

The more your goal has value, importance and impact for you, the more you will be focused on strategies to achieve it and attentive to any opportunity or lead that you pick up that goes in the right direction. Those who deliver results have high levels of motivation to succeed, and great resilience and optimism to overcome challenges, and to work out ways to make it happen. What follows is an example of how to use the linkage tool with a case study of a project setting up a food truck in a university compound, worked on by a group of undergraduate students.

EXAMPLE

You need to organise a food truck at your university as part of an assignment. Your initial thought is that only your grade is really important and so you must just get the work done, nothing more, nothing less. Then you start thinking more deeply. What else could setting up this food truck project bring to you? What opportunities?

Some of these could be for instance:

- When you have set it up, you will need to communicate to the students and professors about it, which may put you in touch with the communications, human resources or catering departments of the university.
- You have always been interested in marketing and communications and would like an internship in this field, so the contacts you might make and the experience of marketing the food truck could be great.
- You will be in touch with many senior administration staff, who each have a professional network.
- You will have to deal with the local authorities to make sure you have all the paperwork done and fulfil health and safety requirements. Knowing some key people in local government could prove useful in terms of experience and networking as you will need to do several internships during your final year.
- You are studying project management in another course, maybe you can use this food truck project to test a new tool. Etc...

Think opportunity!

The 'why' is personal: you choose what – if anything – you will share and communicate. You need to think carefully about this: what you say will always have an influence on how your counterpart views you, on their opinion, and will influence their expectations. Do you want to take the risk of

3.4

WHY DO I WANT WHAT I WANT?

• *GOOD GRADES*
• *LEARN PROJECT MANAGEMENT*
• *GET CONTACTS FOR INTERNSHIP*
• *NETWORKING OPPORTUNITIES*
• *HELP FIND A JOB FOR A FRIEND*
• *HELP REFUGEES LEARN A SKILL*

**I WANT TO SET UP
A FOOD TRUCK**

IDEAS TO GET WHAT I WANT

• *CHECK WITH LOCAL AUTHORITY RE RIGHTS*
• *SURVEY N STUDENTS EATING ON SITE*
• *CHECK WITH SCHOOL ON
EXCLUSIVITY RIGHTS WITH EXISTING CAFETERIA*
• *FIND OUT AVAILABLE BUDGET*
• *PLAN FOR POTENTIAL FUNDING PARTNERS*

having a confrontation about the reasons why you want something, or a debate on whether your reasons are valid? Or do you decide instead that it might be more strategic to mention one specific reason because you are sure that your counterpart is sensitive to the subject? You may even choose to say nothing about your motivations.

EXAMPLE

Helmut is fundraising for a project in the field of cancer research and has contacted the SaveLives Foundation, which is involved in funding large medical research projects.

Helmut feels his project is aligned with its mission and thus will mention his 'one level up', i.e. the first reason why he is contacting them, which is because the project he is fundraising for could lead to a cutting-edge discovery in the field of breast cancer detection. If, on the other hand, Helmut is contacting a private bank, he may choose to talk more about the visibility of the research (for marketing purposes) – thus giving information that could create interest in the other party.

It may not always be necessary to communicate what is in the top of the funnel (motivation), in fact most often it may even be best not to. This is because your reasons *why* belong only to you and may be neither interesting nor useful to share with the other party.

- The more you want to share lines of reasoning, the more you risk trying to convince the other with your own arguments. Your reasons *why* may not make sense or be meaningful to them. The more arguments you give, the higher the risk that the other may not agree with one of your lines of reasoning and that you start debating who is right and who is wrong. Furthermore, the more the other party realizes the object under discussion is important to you the more likely the 'price' goes up.
- You do not necessarily need to be in agreement on the '*why*' to agree with the '*what*'.
- The more you try to convince someone, the more you talk. The more you talk, the less the other talks, the less you listen and learn what has a value for them; which is ultimately what you need to know in order to be able to start the dynamics of exchange.

You thus need to clearly separate your motivations and values (non-negotiable) from your strategies (negotiable); and remember your goal is equally non-negotiable. Being clear on these three will strengthen your confidence, resilience and communication.

Your opening point: your goal

In the linkage tool (Figure 3.3) your goal is positioned in the centre of your analysis, between both funnels. The positioning of your goal is fundamental. It is what will be communicated (see the 'opening statement', page 85) to the other party. Too high a goal and you are talking about your motivations and values, too low and you are talking about your solutions and conditions (*how you imagine that your goal should be reached*). Always test your goal by moving up several levels, asking yourself '*Why do I want this?*' and answering in an honest way. Thinking about the intention behind a goal can also be useful. More on setting your goal will be discussed in Chapter 5.

Your goal is your *opening point*: the point beyond which you open to the other party, to their possible solutions, to suggestions on how you could achieve this, to their reactions to your ideas. *You open to the other*, meaning that beyond this point, the other has a certain amount of *power and influence* over how things will be done – even though ultimately you have the final decision. You can always say no.

Coming back to the *what*, individuals who have the ability to be focused on the end result (or solution focused) can visualize what they want for themselves, their project, their organization. Individuals who have a clear focus are more successful in achieving their goals. Without goals, there is little motivation. Having a clear vision of your goal makes it easier to advance towards it, because goals direct your actions and influence your creativity as you open and seek ways to reach them.

The focus, drive and clear direction that come from having a specific goal is often what makes the difference between those who succeed and those who struggle. Writing about motivation, goal-setting and leaders, professional coach Stephen Gribben points out that:

> Individuals who set goals are easily distinguished from others by their level of motivation and sense of purpose in what they do. Individuals and teams that are focused on their goals rise to every challenge and create opportunities to achieve their desired outcomes. Those who do not set goals can only drift in the hope that they will end up somewhere better.[7]

Over recent years neuroscientific research has looked into the link between goal-setting and the brain. As Chowdhury reports, Granot *et al* found that goal-setting gives a boost to systolic blood pressure, which brings about action, and Alvarez and Emory noted that the reticular activating system (RAS) is a part of the brain that plays a crucial role in regulating goal-setting actions.[8] The RAS processes all the information and sensory channels related to the things that need attention right now. Therefore when you set a goal, and it would seem especially when you write with pen and paper, your RAS is activated. And one of the things your RAS does when activated is to filter the messages and information you receive from your environment, only registering the information related to what you are paying attention to at this specific moment in time. Therefore the RAS activation helps focus the mind to concentrate on those pieces of information that are related to the goals you have set out to achieve.

As mentioned earlier, when it comes to goal-setting, the RAS functions in two ways: first by the simple act of writing your goal down, and second through visualization. Imagination is essential when it comes to goal-setting. Berkman and Lieberman reported that people who have the power to visualize their goals have a higher activation at the brain level. Repeatedly imaging success and reminding yourself of your aim maintains a steady stimulation in the RAS and promotes effective goal-setting.[9]

So, make an appointment with yourself and put aside some special time to think clearly about what you want to achieve.

Another advantage of carefully using the linkage tool is that it may actually clarify at times that what you really want is to convince the other party that your idea or solution to a specific problem is the best one. This will help you realize that your best strategy should not be negotiation, but actually finding clear, well-thought arguments aimed to convince.

EXAMPLE

Jerry is an IT business analyst in a large cooperation. She has been working on a specific challenge for some time now: her internal customer – the customer support centre – has a problem monitoring customers' complaints. Jerry believes she has finally found the best solution with the IT software development group: a new module to install on the existing application. She has several strategies she can implement with the customer support centre:

1   To convince them: '*I have found the best solution and I will give you all the arguments to convince you about this so that we can go ahead with the update.*'

2   To negotiate: First Jerry has to do her linkage and 'go up one level', i.e. from '*I want to install module X*' she asks herself '*Why do I want to install module X?*' One answer would be '*To respond to my business unit's needs to monitor customer complaints*'. Her goal then becomes '*I want to improve monitoring of customer complaints*' and to discuss the conditions under which we can implement a satisfying solution to both you (internal customer) and the company. '*I have an idea to present, but there may be others...*'

The first option involves Jerry convincing her customer that her solution is the most efficient and best one.

For the second option Jerry puts the focus on finding a solution and on the characteristics this solution should have.

The first option is outlined in Figure 3.5. The second option would look something like Figure 3.6.

JERRY'S TWO OPTIONS
OPTION 1

3.5

WHY?

- EASY TO INSTALL
- SUPPORTED BY CUSTOM SYSTEM
- ANSWERS NEED X
- ...

Moving from

I WANT TO INSTALL MODULE X

to

HOW

- SET UP PROJECT
- PLAN SYSTEM UPGRADE
- FIND RESOURCES TO TEST
- ...

OPTION 2

3.6

WHY

- TO RESPOND TO CUSTOMER SERVICE NEEDS
- TO GAUGE RELIABLE NEEDS
- ...

Moving from

I WANT TO MONITOR CUSTOMER COMPLAINTS

to

HOW

- A NEW APPLICATION OR AN EXISTING UPGRADE TO THE EXISTING ONE
- CLEARLY DEFINED SPECIFICATION
- DEFINE BUDGET

Remember, **negotiation is a choice,** and in some situations you will need another approach, such as in the above example when what you really want is to *convince* your customer to let you install Module X. Time pressure could also influence your choice of tactics. The important thing is to ask yourself the questions, do your linkage and give it some serious thought. And if you make the decision to negotiate, i.e. if you enter into a bilateral process, *you must listen to and take into account the wishes and needs of the other party.*

Having the right opening level when you do finally meet the other party will widen your choices, create more opportunities for creativity and help you position yourself correctly.

Volition and preparation

Many studies and real-life situations have highlighted the fact that the most common reasons people do not achieve what they want is:

- because they are not clear on what they actually want
- because they do not dare ask for what they want
- because even if they do ask for something, their message is often confused and misunderstood

First and foremost, why is it so important to know what you want? Have you ever tried playing darts blindfolded? Except by pure chance there is little hope that you will reach a target you cannot see or visualize. Furthermore, it will be extremely challenging to communicate a goal clearly when it is not well defined in your own mind. The more your goal is clear and meaningful for you, the more it will come across clearly to the other and the more you will actually dare to ask; your (self) confidence level will be heightened and so will your resilience.

Volition is fundamental because it is so strongly linked with the realization of a goal. Author and Buddhist Joseph Goldstein remarks on the importance of actually wanting something, on the power of will. 'It's like the chief of staff of the mind, coordinating all the other factors to accomplish a purpose... its function is to organize, gather, and direct all the other mental factors for a particular end'.[10] Having a goal that is clear in your mind and that you can put into words is fundamental to being able to reach it: as soon as it requires the help of others, you must be able to communicate it.

Willpower and intention carry the force of action. In other words, all intentional, volitional actions have the power to bring about results in the present and in future.

Because motivation plays such a determining role in how our lives unfold, a strong and inspiring goal is a basis to the five-step negotiation process that is described in this book. A lot of individuals, when asked, find it incredibly difficult to state clearly what they want to achieve, to actually voice the desired result or solution. And if you cannot say what you want, in a negotiation process that involves by nature one or more 'other parties', how are they going to know? Some try lengthy manipulative strategies, which can at times work, but at what price? You want to build and negotiate partnerships and collaborations that will last. How likely is your counterpart going to follow the agreement or continue with the relationship if they have been manipulated in the process? It is far more efficient at many levels to express clearly what one wants (see Chapter 6) in a transparent way, being clear on the fact that transparency does not mean giving away or giving up. Transparency rather than secrecy often has a disarming effect.

Once you have understood and adopted the mindset described in the previous chapter, and you have a clear view of your goal and your motivations (having done a linkage on your goal), there are five specific steps to practise solution-focused negotiation. Each step is distinct and separate, with its own tool and method. This separation is important as it helps to be systematic and clarifies behaviour. Each will be described in detail in the following chapters.

Chapter 3: summary points

- To be able to enter into a negotiation process you need volition and opportunity (i.e. for you to want to negotiate is not enough: your volition must also correspond to the volition of the other party: all must want to engage). The other two prerequisites are creativity and flexibility.
- By being creative you will open the scope of what you will be able to achieve and increase the result of your negotiations. Widening the options of what you could ask for, allied with flexibility, will ensure your negotiated agreement has more value and content.

- Throughout the entire process maintaining interest, not only yours but also the interest of all involved parties, is key. However remember at all times that the various parties do not need to share the same interest, and beware of falling into the common trap of trying to argue your point and getting them to agree that your interest is more worthwhile than theirs.

- Interest is a fundamental concept. Although the various parties do not need to share the same interest, it is really important that each one has theirs taken into account.

- Using the linkage tool will help you reflect on what you want, on why you want it and on the possible strategies to get there.

- Your goal is your entry point to the negotiation, the point beyond which you need to take the other party into account.

Notes

1 Ayelet Fishbach, quoted in A G Walton. What happened to your goals? Chicago Booth Review, 2017. https://review.chicagobooth.edu/behavioral-science/2017/article/what-happened-your-goals?source=ic-em- (archived at https://perma.cc/STX2-LMRQ)

2 M R Chowdhury. The science and psychology of goal-setting 101, *Positive Psychology*, 2020. https://positivepsychology.com/goal-setting-psychology/ (archived at https://perma.cc/A4YC-PFYX)

3 Ayelet Fishbach, quoted in A G Walton. What happened to your goals? Chicago Booth Review, 2017. https://review.chicagobooth.edu/behavioral-science/2017/article/what-happened-your-goals?source=ic-em- (archived at https://perma.cc/STX2-LMRQ)

4 M R Chowdhury. The science and psychology of goal-setting 101, *Positive Psychology*, 2020. https://positivepsychology.com/goal-setting-psychology/ (archived at https://perma.cc/A4YC-PFYX)

5 Ayelet Fishbach, quoted in A G Walton. What happened to your goals? Chicago Booth Review, 2017. https://review.chicagobooth.edu/behavioral-science/2017/article/what-happened-your-goals?source=ic-em- (archived at https://perma.cc/STX2-LMRQ)

6 C D Kerns. The positive psychology approach to goal management: Applying positive psychology to goal management increases effectiveness, *Graziadio Business Review*, 8 (3). https://gbr.pepperdine.edu/2010/08/the-positive-psychology-approach-to-goal-management/ (archived at https://perma.cc/JAV5-8CZW)

7 S Gribben (2016) *Key Coaching Models: The 70+ models every manager and coach needs to know*, Financial Times Publishing, London

8 M R Chowdhury. The science and psychology of goal-setting 101, *Positive Psychology*, 2020. https://positivepsychology.com/goal-setting-psychology/ (archived at https://perma.cc/A4YC-PFYX)

9 M R Chowdhury. The science and psychology of goal-setting 101, *Positive Psychology*, 2020. https://positivepsychology.com/goal-setting-psychology/ (archived at https://perma.cc/A4YC-PFYX)

10 J Goldstein (2013) *Mindfulness*, Sounds True, Louisville, CO

Preparation

Part Two of this book focuses on the aspects of the five-step negotiation process that involve preparation and includes both the 'contextual analysis' and the 'goal analysis'. These areas of focus must be considered in advance of negotiations and appropriate time should be allocated to these two steps. Benjamin Franklin is widely attributed with the adage that by failing to prepare you are preparing to fail. He was right. Preparation is a fundamental prerequisite to a good worthwhile negotiation.

Part Two begins with a chapter on contextual analysis and will explain how to consider and evaluate the context in which your negotiations will take place and how to plan accordingly. This involves externally orientated topics such as the overall context, organization and planning. Following on from this, the next chapter on goal analysis will expand upon how to prepare your goal and your negotiation roadmap. This involves internally orientated topics such as what you wish to achieve (your goal and your conditions). Both of these steps contain checklists and tools to help you through your analysis. Once these steps are established, Part Three will continue with an overview of the encounter, and Part Four with building an offer and clinching a deal, as well as the final step of implementation.

04

Step 1: contextual analysis

This chapter focuses on contextual analysis and the necessary elements that need to be thought about during this step of the process. It is important that each element is thought about and, for many, decided upon. The more you know about the situation and the overall context, the more you will be able to think about what you want to achieve, choose your best negotiating team members, clarify whom you should be trying to get in touch with to bring to the negotiating table and plan how to establish contact with them. Being familiar with and knowledgeable about the context will make you feel more comfortable with the negotiation at hand. A solid understanding and prepa-ration will ensure you are and act more competent, that you are quicker to understand and take on board new elements, and will have an impact on your self-confidence.

This chapter begins by exploring in detail what gave rise to the overall desire or need to negotiate and analysing the context in which the negotia-tions are to take place. Who your best interlocutors are – these represent your counterparts, the people, parties, communities, etc, that you will want or need to have at the negotiation table – and how to reach out to them together with who should make up your own negotiation team will be covered. Information sharing and gathering has an important and at times crucial influence, whether it is the information you choose to share or the questions you decide to ask. Logistical and planning aspects will also need to be carefully thought about.

We then discuss multicultural negotiations. Multicultural negotiations are an important consideration in your contextual analysis. We operate in a truly global world. Negotiations are no longer limited to who you can see across the table or reach on the phone and it is becoming easier – even vital – to develop partnerships with people all over the world. However, cultural norms, best practices and etiquette vary and their impact on negotiations and communication should never be understated. Although the same methodology can be applied to all cultures, there are elements that you need to take into account or you will undoubtedly experience difficulties. Multicultural negotiations require extra care and understanding, which is why a whole section has been dedicated to this topic.

Contextual analysis

The contextual analysis helps you to reflect on the context in which the negotiations are to happen. It will help you to decide whether negotiation is the best approach, to understand what gave rise to the situation or conflict and to elaborate a macro strategy. It will assist you in determining the environment in which the meetings will (hopefully) take place, the logistics, as well as the crucial aspects pertaining to information. It will also help you to think about who will be involved.

The following themes/issues must be thought through and *where relevant* answered. In many political and business situations, each specific point can in itself be a negotiation and have high stakes.

Once you are clear on what you want to achieve from this negotiation, on your goal and wishes related to this goal, you need to carefully think about the following points.

Context

The first consideration in the contextual analysis is to understand what gave rise to the need or desire to negotiate. Context refers to the circumstances that surround and influence situations. In certain situations, the context will have a minor impact, though still be relevant; however, in other situations it may be hugely influential. At times context can be quite straightforward, as when negotiating how to go to your daughter's birthday party without hindering the advancement of a work project (see Chapter 1) and at times incredibly complex, as in the Brexit negotiations.

The following should be kept in mind when analysing the setting:

- What is the overall context in which the negotiation is going to take place (political situation, social conflict, economic issues, merger, project management, etc)?
- What is your high-level goal and do you think negotiation is the best strategy?
- Do you think there may be hidden agendas? Do *you* have any hidden agendas? What is your real intention?

Timing and planning

The next element to be carefully thought about is the overall timing, schedule and planning of the negotiation, particularly with regards to planning the encounters. It is important to leave sufficient time for several encounters and for people to think about the negotiations and take into account new elements or changes of circumstances. At times your negotiation timeframe will be open ended and at times there will be a deadline when you know that by a specific date an agreement needs to have been found. For instance negotiations around the issue of accommodation for young athletes in the case of the Youth Olympic Games that took place in Lausanne, Switzerland needed to be finalized before the beginning of the games in January 2020, a fixed deadline date.

The following questions need to be answered:

- When should the negotiations take place? When is the best moment to enter into discussion?
- Are there any deadlines or milestones you need to take into account? In some situations, a deadline exists, in which case you need to plan from the end date (e.g. a football World Cup: the start date is non-negotiable; the construction of an Olympic village needs to be finished before the start of the games; a module needs to be developed before the software can go live). In these situations you need to do some retro-planning and start with the end date in mind, planning backwards.

- What is the best time for the meetings to happen? Seek good timing, when attention and readiness are likely to be highest. Make sure you plan sufficient time and sufficient meetings. There can be – and often are – several encounters ('rounds of negotiations' – as it is an iterative process), as mentioned in Chapter 2.

- How many meetings do you think there will be? Plan ahead to lessen the risk of pressure on both parties. It is rare that people react well and creatively under pressure.

- How long should the overall process last? And each meeting?

EXAMPLE

A factory is closing down in 24 months' time. A collective labour agreement needs to be negotiated for the workers. The agreement needs to be accepted first by staff and trade union members, then by the CEO before the legal aspects can be drawn up. It is therefore important to plan specific milestones well in advance, i.e. by the end of the first quarter the proposal is drafted and sent to the CEO, by the second week of the second quarter the updated proposal is worked on and submitted. By the end of the third quarter a definite proposal is made by the legal department. By mid fourth quarter the plan and agreement are communicated to all staff and to the outside world.

Interlocutor, communication style and cultural differences

The third topic to be considered concerns your counterparts – those people who you ideally have at the negotiating table. Talking to the 'right' person is one big step towards achieving your goal. You will need to clarify who has the most power or influence to help you, directly or indirectly, establish how to get into contact with them and gather as much information about them as possible, such as their preferred communication means, their professional profile and their cultural background.

The following points will need to be clarified:

- Who would your best interlocutor be, your ideal counterpart? It is very important to identify and ensure that the right people are at the table and that you have targeted the best person for you, *considering the topic to be discussed.*[1] What authority, hierarchy and power of decision or circle of influence do they have?

- What do you think their interest may be (based on facts)? Avoid guessing and imagination: if hypotheses are made, make sure they are validated.

- Are there any cultural differences of which you should be aware?

- What do you know about their preferred communication style (e.g. face-to-face or electronic?)[2] How accessible are they? What do you need to do to enter into contact with them? Can you call or email them directly or would it be better if you had an introduction?

- What is your past (if any) relationship with the other party and how will this influence the process?

> EXAMPLE
>
> When negotiating a collective labour agreement is it best to talk first to the head of HR or to the CEO? Is one more likely to be open to the staff situation than the other? Does one have influence on the other?

Location, access and logistics

It might be necessary to consider logistical and organizational aspects so that you prepare for various alternatives. Depending on the context, this might have a big impact, for instance on planning (see page 85). For instance if your negotiations involve people from different countries who would need to get together in physical presence, you will need to plan for more time to allow for travel. Or if the encounters are to be solely organized through videoconferencing applications (see Chapter 8 on online negotiations), you will need to take into careful consideration access to technology and bandwidth. At times, specific equipment might be required; it may be that special security access codes will be needed to enter a classified building or laboratory. In some peace- and conflict-related situations, decisions pertaining to whether or not the various parties can be armed when they meet will need to be agreed on.

Careful analysis of the following will help:

- Where should the negotiations and encounters take place? Try to make sure the location is suitable and carefully chosen, with little noise or distraction. Layout and comfort are important to create an atmosphere conducive to good and effective communication. Avoid all negative influences in the environment.
- Are there any security issues you should take into account (e.g. access restrictions, war zones, health hazard zones)?[3] Does anything need to be taken into account concerning access and location (for instance, the last meeting happened in a neutral location, or in my counterpart's town/country, so should this one be in yours...)?
- Is any specific equipment needed?

For online requirements see Chapter 8.

Your negotiation team

When negotiating, it is usually helpful to work in a well-prepared team. Although people can and do negotiate alone – at times there is no other option – being surrounded by and part of a knowledgeable team can be extremely useful. This element of your contextual analysis focuses on who should be on your negotiation team. A crowd rarely equates with efficiency. The team is made up of several specific roles and always includes two main people (a 'pilot' and a 'co-pilot'). Several experts can also be necessary. At times you might also require an interpreter. The role breakdown is as follows:

- *Pilot:* Their main tasks are to lead the discussion, to talk, ask questions, answer, give information, make hypothetical proposals.
- *Co-pilot:* Their main tasks are to observe, reformulate if something is unclear, help stay on track, take notes and make summaries.
- *Experts:* Their main tasks are to give their expert opinion and advice on specific matters and answer questions pertaining to their area of expertise.
- *Interpreter:* In multicultural negotiations and in negotiations where there might be people who are deaf and/or dumb, it may be necessary to have interpreters present. These need a full briefing about the subject of the

discussion so that they can prepare the terminology prior to the meeting. In multicultural negotiations it is important to have access to an interpreter familiar with the culture in and with which you are negotiating.[4] Choose your interpreter wisely. Before hiring interpreters, determine their experience and skill and be sure to brief them before negotiations start. Manage and plan for interpretation like you would any other tactical element in deal-making. You will also need to bear in mind if the interpreting is going to be done simultaneously or consecutively and adapt the installation accordingly.

The pilot/co-pilot function as a team, with the co-pilot helping the pilot when necessary, reading the cues, pitching in when something needs clarifying, providing the pilot with space to think. It is almost always best to be a team (i.e. pilot/co-pilot) if possible – it helps having four eyes observing and four ears listening; it reduces pressure and gives each member some breathing/thinking space. For instance, when the co-pilot makes a summary, the pilot can check in on their notes to see what still needs to be discussed and concentrate on the way forward. It is obviously not always possible for there to be two people negotiating, as for instance in a job interview. However even if you are alone, the above duties need to be carried out: at times you will take on the pilot role, and at times the co-pilot role, asking for a few minutes to summarize and read through your notes.

The role of expert is often necessary and important; however, experts have to be carefully monitored and asked to respond only to specific questions. Indeed, the best way to kill a negotiation is to put two experts face to face, because experts function with a logic of truth ('*I am right*'), whereas negotiators function with a logic of interest. Experts 'know best' (after all they *are* experts) and tend to argue their point. However, think about it: *is it more important for you to get what you want or to be right? Is your ego possibly getting in the way?* Ideally the experts are not in the same room as the negotiators, but it should be possible to reach them at short notice and they should be clearly briefed on their role and what is expected from them, i.e. only to answer precise questions or give information when specifically asked.

Professional negotiator Laurent Combalbert[5] strongly advocates that the person who is ultimately going to decide, the person who has the strongest interest that the agreement is negotiated, should in fact avoid being pilot, or even being present, but should instead delegate the discussions and negotiations to someone else. It is best to avoid having someone with an inflated ego at the negotiation table, or if this person must be present then ensure you brief them carefully about the advantages *they have* in remaining seemingly more passive.

During the stages of contextual analysis, decide who will be pilot, and who will be co-pilot. These roles are interchangeable, but you cannot be both at the same time. It is advisable to prepare the roles beforehand, so that you are clear when you get to the negotiation table as to who does what, and how to communicate with one another. Make sure the team is well briefed and that they never contradict each other in front of the other participants to the meetings. Roles and responsibilities must be clear, and personal opinions avoided: you are a team and need to function as one, particularly when facing your counterparts.

Finally, outline what authority and power of decision you and your team have.

Information

Information is crucial and has an influence on which way the negotiation is going to evolve. The quality, relevance and availability of information for each party need to be carefully checked. Everyone must have *the information they require* to be able to make a balanced decision. The risk of a decision or commitment backfiring because it was based on inadequate or insufficient information is high. In some situations, retention of data or giving false information is used to threaten deals or manipulate the other party. If you enter into this game, what likelihood is there that the person will respect the negotiated agreement? And if that reason alone is not enough, remember that at times hiding information can be legally damaging. The commitment of all parties is needed to make a lasting, successful partnership and to put into effect the negotiated agreement: if they find out they have been 'had' or manipulated, how likely are they to put energy into the partnership? You need to consider two aspects:

- *What do you need to know about the other party and the situation?* It is important to find out as much as possible about the other's context. Nowadays, with the internet, there is a wealth of information around (annual reports, budget analysis, social networks, documents, articles, etc), as well as people and colleagues who may know about the people, culture and organizations with which you are about to deal. The more you know, the more you can understand the subtleties of the situation. Beware, however, that not all you might find reflects the truth.

  If in doubt, do not imagine or make assumptions; instead validate your hypotheses or simply ask questions. Information gathering is even more important when the parties are multicultural, e.g. to be aware of the rules of behaviour of the other cultures present. Carefully prepare what you need to ask to gather information that you could not find alone, keeping in mind your real intention. This helps avoid leading questions and hidden motives.

- *What is it in your interest that they know about you? What do you want them to know about you and your situation?* Many negotiation techniques hold on to to the notion that 'the less the other knows the better'. The model described in this book is, however, built along the lines that information strategically given plays an extremely important role in creating interest and at times even a need for the other party to negotiate. The idea behind giving information about you or your situation is to create and/or influence *their* interest in striking a deal with you; in other words, for them to realize there is something for them to gain in building this puzzle, in engaging in the negotiation, in collaborating in this issue or partnership.

    There are two basic rules to follow: first, everything you say must be true, and second, you do not need to say everything – you choose selectively what you say. Do not hide the difficulties. Being transparent can have a disarming effect.[6]

The power of information is not to be underestimated. To go one step further and deeper, you can also ask yourself what your real intention is behind the information you want to give.

INFORMATION IS STRATEGIC

4.2

TO SHARE

Whatever you say must be true – but you need not say everything

WHAT IT IS IN YOUR INTEREST TO SHARE WITH THE OTHER ABOUT YOU AND THE SITUATION

TO FIND OUT

Prepare useful relevant questions

WHAT YOU NEED TO KNOW THAT YOU COULDN'T FIND OUT ALONE

Multicultural negotiations

Various studies have shown that negotiations across cultures are most often more challenging than negotiations conducted within the same culture, mainly because cultures are characterized by different behaviours and attitudes, communication styles and value systems. Culture encompasses the social behaviours and norms found in human societies, as well as the knowledge, beliefs, arts, laws, customs, capabilities and habits of the individuals in these groups.[7] When researching how culture and race shape gender dynamics in negotiations[8] (more about gender and negotiations will be discussed in Chapter 12), Toosi *et al* consider culture as being a larger network of behavioural patterns and values, which, together with race and gender, interact to shape conceptions of socially acceptable behaviours in negotiations. Culture is therefore not limited to nationality but to any group of people who share similar behaviours, values, norms and communication style.

Culture plays an important role in negotiations, because people's culture makes up the lenses through which the attitudes and actions of others are perceived and interpreted and through which they see and interpret the world that surrounds them. Behaviours, norms, values and communication styles are highly influenced by cultural differences, and the potential for misunderstandings is high, which can have costly consequences. When even within the same culture people can perceive and interpret the 'same' reality differently, there is significant potential for differences when dealing with several cultures simultaneously. Furthermore, not only do countries have unique cultures, but teams and organizations do too. Often people tend to think of culture as being linked only to nationality, but increasingly culture spans a much wider meaning, such as organizational culture, village culture, university culture, prison culture, teenager culture and deaf and dumb culture.[9]

4.3   *CULTURE IS A SYSTEM OF NORMS, BEHAVIOURS AND VALUES SHARED BY MEMBERS OF A GROUP WHICH INFLUENCES COMMUNICATION STYLE.*

BEWARE
OF STEREOTYPES AND ASSUMPTIONS AS THEY MAY LEAD TO COSTLY MISUNDERSTANDINGS.

Multicultural negotiations are more challenging for three main reasons:

- Stereotypes are often present when dealing with different cultures, and can often be pejorative and lead to distorted expectations and misinterpretations.

- Others' behaviours, values and beliefs are interpreted through the lens of one's own culture.

- Culture highly influences communication styles.

To simplify, humans organize data into 'little boxes' called stereotypes, which are cognitive shortcuts that help people organize the mass of data they constantly face. Stereotypes help classify people and behaviours. Still simplifying, assumptions are then made, based on behaviour, which are then interpreted in a specific way. In other words, what someone says or how they behave is interpreted based on assumptions that are justified by stereotypes – many of which are linked to culture.

Dutch psychologist Hofstede[10] noted in his research that cultural values structure perceptions and considerably influence communication styles, whether verbal or non-verbal. Various communication styles have developed throughout history and cultures. Recognizing different styles and respecting them is a first step to improve multicultural communication. A second step is to know how to adapt and change one's listening so as to understand *the meaning behind the message*. No one style is better than the other, no one perception is more correct than the other. Just like verbal communication, non-verbal communication is highly influenced by differences in cultures. One common example is eye contact: in certain communities eye contact is a sign of honesty and respect, whilst in others eye contact is considered a sign of threat and challenge.

Although cultural differences can bring additional challenges and difficulties to reaching an agreement in negotiations, they can also be fantastic opportunities for thinking about creative and valuable elements, due to different perceptions, priorities, beliefs and values.[11]

While there is no simple answer to these multicultural challenges, the following tips can help:

- Become more conscious of the (at times subtle) variety of cultures around the negotiation table. Before any negotiation, take time to study the context and the other party, including the various cultures to which they belong – nationality, field of work, corporate culture, etc. Learn as much as possible.

- Adapt your style to the context – as long as it is not a compromise on your values. For instance in certain cultures there may be certain (to you) submissive behaviours that are unacceptable to you. In this case you might want to ask yourself if it is not better for you to send someone else to the negotiation table.
- Seek to understand what underlies the codes of behaviour.
- When negotiating in multicultural environments, remember:
  o All perceptions are relative and incomplete.
  o All perceptions are justified and acceptable: forget the assumption that your perception is universal.
- If you feel respected in your cultural differences, you will feel more inclined to respect the other.
- To open up to the other party's perception does not mean abandoning one's own perception, but widening it, building on it and possibility even adapting it.
- Observe without judging.
- Ask if in doubt.
- Each party needs the other party's help: each one is an opportunity for the other. It is thus in your interest to understand them as best as possible.
- You are not there to judge and change others' behaviours.

4.4   **SOME TIPS TO KEEP IN MIND**

*FORGET THE ASSUMPTION
'MY PERCEPTION IS UNIVERSAL'.*

*LEARN AS MUCH AS POSSIBLE ABOUT THE
CULTURES YOU ARE DEALING WITH.*

*OBSERVE WITH AN OPEN MIND –
AVOIDING (OR BEING AWARE OF) JUDGEMENT.*

WHEN POSSIBLE, ADAPT STYLE TO CONTEXT.

*CROSS-CULTURAL NEGOTIATIONS HAVE
A HUGE POTENTIAL FOR CREATIVITY, AND
FOR CAPITALIZING ON DIFFERENT PRIORITIES,
VALUES AND PREFERENCES*

*WHATEVER CULTURE THEY COME FROM,
YOU NEED THE OTHER PARTY TO REACH
AN AGREEMENT.*

Fundamentally, if you negotiate an agreement in a multicultural setting, you must abandon the idea that your perceptions are universally shared and that your interpretations are self-evident. The main question is not *'who is right'* or *'who is wrong'*, but rather *'How can we take all interests into account and negotiate a sustainable deal, considering we are fundamentally different?'* Multicultural negotiations, whilst being more challenging than mono-cultural negotiations, also bring a huge potential for creativity, which helps find more varied conditions, thus increasing the capacity for exchange.

A few words on humour

Humour is often linked with causing amusement or laughter about a trait or a (sub)culture in another person or group. In other words, humour and jokes often make fun of stereotypical attributes. Attempts at humour should be avoided as this can be a minefield, and a highly risky enterprise, especially in multicultural negotiation. You might seriously damage the relationship, you might upset someone you need, you might give a sorry image of yourself as being, for instance, insensitive. What you think is genuinely funny may turn out to be (highly) offensive to the recipient. A self-deprecating joke might be possible if you think carefully about the effect you might have: what is your real intention? Do you really need to joke to warm the atmosphere? Anything involving politics, religion or sexuality is obviously also off-limits![12]

The contextual analysis worksheet

The worksheet below can be used to help prepare your contextual analysis. It is to be used as a checklist – only filling in boxes where relevant, depending on the situation. Go through the worksheet, starting with the first column (*Desired conditions*), and always start with the ideal situation for you, if you had a choice. In other words, if you could choose location, where would the meeting take place? If you could choose the people who would attend (both in your team and your counterparts), who would you choose? *Known elements* refer to any element that you know about the situation, and that you think relevant. *Unacceptable conditions* are elements that are not acceptable for you. Say, for instance, that you can have that meeting you seek, but only if you fly to Sweden for a one-hour encounter. This might simply not be acceptable for you.

TABLE 4.1

Aim (macro level)			
	Desired conditions (what I really would like)	Known elements	Unacceptable conditions
Interlocutor: name, function, power/influence...			
Cultural aspects to bear in mind (e.g. possible need for interpreter)			
Timing, planning and possible deadlines			
Location and access			
Logistical and security issues			
My team: who, what roles, any need for experts, what authority			
Communication style and used media			
Information: to find out, to ask, to give			

Chapter 4: summary points

- Analysing in detail the context in which your negotiations will take place plays a very important role.

- Start the process with a macro analysis, a big picture view of the setting in which you are called on to negotiate.

- Each element of the contextual analysis can be extremely important and in itself be a separate negotiation. You should take the time it needs to be clear on each one.

- Base what you can on facts rather than assumptions and imagination, and find out as much as possible. When in doubt, prepare questions.

- Your negotiation team will need to be briefed carefully on their roles, on what is expected from them and on how you want to communicate between yourselves. Pilots and co-pilots play an active and important role.

- Be highly vigilant when negotiating in multicultural environments as they can be exceptionally challenging and sensitive. Multiculturalism also gives tremendous potential for creativity, so remain open-minded and learn as much as possible.

- Avoid humour as the risk of creating embarrassment and blockage outweighs the potentially positive effect.

Notes

1 One big problem for the French government with the 'Gilet Jaunes' conflict in France end 2018 and early 2019 was the lack of a specific interlocutor representative of the movement with whom the French government could talk. *Le Point*, 17 January 2019, n 2420

2 Negotiation skills: Negotiation strategies and negotiation techniques to help you become a better negotiator, from the Program on Negotiation at Harvard Law School, consulted November 2019

3 Many issues needed careful planning and negotiating in order to organize the June 2018 summit that happened between US President Donald Trump and North Korean leader Kim Jong-un. For instance, the location of the summit was thoroughly negotiated, including security, access, geography, etc.

4   Harvard Law School (nd) *International Negotiations: Cross-cultural communication skills for international business executives.* www.pon.harvard. edu/freemium/international-negotiations-cross-cultural-communication-skills-for-international-business-executives/ (archived at https://perma.cc/9237-L9Z8)

5   L Combalbert. *Le Point*, 17 January 2019, n 2420

6   B Piccard. How to raise $170 million for a crazy idea, 2016. https://www. linkedin.com/pulse/how-raise-170-million-crazy-idea-bertrand-piccard (archived at https://perma.cc/U3YA-2VR9)

7   Culture, Wikipedia.en.wikipedia.org/wiki/Culture (archived at https://perma. cc/U3YA-2VR9)

8   N R Toosi, Z Semnani-Azad, W Shen, S Mor and E T Amanatullah (2020) How culture and race shape gender dynamics in negotiations, in *Research Handbook on Gender and Negotiation*, ed M Olekalns and J A Kennedy, Edward Elgar, Cheltenham. www.researchgate.net/publication/340249117_ How_Culture_and_Race_Shape_Gender_Dynamics_in_Negotiations (archived at https://perma.cc/GS6H-8MJT)

9   L Cardenas. Overcoming cultural barriers in negotiations and the importance of communication in international business deals, Harvard Law School, 27 April 2021. www.pon.harvard.edu/daily/international-negotiation-daily/ bridging-the-cultural-divide-in-international-business-negotiations/ (archived at https://perma.cc/E5SY-ADTU)

10 G Hofstede (2001) *Culture's Consequences: Comparing values, behaviors, institutions and organizations across nations*, SAGE, New York

11 Inspired by F Gino. Dear negotiation coach: Crossing cultures in negotiation, *Negotiation*, September 2013. www.pon.harvard.edu/ (archived at https:// perma.cc/CL3E-YTBQ)

12 For further reading on humour, see M Young, Whimsicality: The power of humor in negotiation, 2016. www.linkedin.com/pulse/whimsicality-power-humor-negotiation-mark-young (archived at https://perma.cc/F5W6-KT7H)

05

Step 2: goal analysis

This chapter focuses on one of the most important elements of your negotiation: your goal, the end result your negotiation seeks to achieve. You will examine how to analyse in detail what you want to accomplish and the purpose of the negotiation. Starting with your overall aim – which would have been clarified using the linkage tool seen in Chapter 3 – you will be taken through the elements that will make up your negotiation roadmap.

To begin with, a few common errors to be avoided in this step will be presented. The subsequent three sections then explore what makes up a negotiation roadmap. First, the importance of goal definition and formulation will be discussed. The next focus will be on how to break your goal down into negotiable conditions, and how to decide which ones are vital and which ones are optional. The final section will concentrate on the importance of setting your ambitions and limits on your conditions.

Before you start, find a quiet space and make an appointment with yourself so you have time to actually think what is it you really want to achieve or obtain, and make sure you are fully enclosed in your 'ego bubble'.

Three common errors to avoid

There are several errors people often make when involved in a negotiation, which can have serious consequences on the quality of the negotiated outcome.

Not preparing

The first one is not preparing, or not taking adequate time to clearly think what you want. It is well known that good preparation enhances the probability of a good deal, or even simply of reaching a satisfying agreement in some complex situations. You cannot reach a goal you cannot see, let alone communicate it in a clear and hopefully unambiguous way. And yet many people go into a negotiation with an ill-defined idea of what they actually want. Taking the time out to think clearly pays back the investment.

Being reactive

The second error is being reactive. You should (try to) never react directly to what the other party asks for, or to the circumstances. Reacting often leads you to overlook what *you* actually want, to forget yourself, and pushes you to act mainly based on another person's request, influenced by what *they* want. Remember your counterpart has no room in this second step. During the time you spend preparing and clarifying what you want, you must be enclosed in your ego bubble. You do not think of anyone else – you concentrate only on yourself, which can be your project, your team, your family, your situation, your 'side'. You should always seek to anchor yourself in yourself, and try to change a reactive into a proactive stance – an opportunity. '*If I cannot change this situation, how can I turn it into a possible advantage for me?*' At times you cannot do much about external circumstances, but you can always decide how you are going to react. Your reaction is something you have power over, even if at times this may seem tremendously difficult. This is discussed further in Chapter 9.

EXAMPLE

You are faced with the unfortunate situation of losing your job due to economic reasons.[1] You have several choices:

- You can fight ('*I should not be fired – I will sue you*'), possibly getting a lawyer to represent you or going to a trade union or the media.
- You can feel a victim ('*It is so unfair, I will creep away*').
- Or you can change your mindset and look for the opportunity in a rough situation ('*As I have been made redundant, then I would like to leave under the best conditions possible, and these conditions are...*').

This last option has a huge impact on the dynamics of the discussions you will have with your superiors and your HR department and on the way the people you talk to will respond. And, possibly even more importantly, it will have a big effect on how you view yourself, as you become a more proactive actor, at least trying to affect the outcome, rather than possibly feeling more like a victim and simply accepting what is happening. You then at least open the possibility to be able to negotiate an interesting package. Nelson Mandela summarized this approach by suggesting that choices should *reflect hopes rather than fears.*[2]

Wanting to achieve two things at the same time

The third error to avoid is preparing and mixing two goals at the same time. The risk is that you dilute your energy, creativity and concentration. Time is precious and you will have less of it because you are thinking about and analysing two goals in depth rather than concentrating on your most important aim. Having two aims often entails a 'best' option and a 'second best' option, and you cannot fight for both at the same time. You cannot win a gold medal if you have settled for silver in your mind. Another risk with preparing two goals is that you will tend to – even unconsciously – give the other party the power to decide which one is the most important, when in fact you and only you should decide what your goal and priorities are.

The ideal course of action is finding the one objective that inspires you, that you really want to achieve in partnership with your counterparts.

In another context, with regards to the effort put into one goal, the same idea was described as follows:

> One day a novice archer presented himself with two arrows. His master said to him 'Beginners should not use two arrows. If you rely on the second, you will not give enough attention to the first. On the contrary, it is important to be fully concentrated on the first arrow, not wondering whether it will reach its target.'[3]

Goal analysis

In this step you will prepare your goal in great detail. You will define your conditions, quantify boundaries, describe your strongest desires and breaking points, and finalize the information you wish to give and the questions you need to ask. The tool and roadmap at the end of the chapter will help you carefully detail what you want to achieve.

Your goal is the foundation of your negotiation, your driving force, your direction. For this step to happen in the optimum manner, you must *lock yourself in your 'ego bubble'* (see Chapter 2) and focus on *what you want to achieve*, without wondering what the other party wants or imagining how they may react. If you think about the other party at this point, you will easily downgrade your wishes and best hopes, change some aspects of your aim, or even ignore some things of importance to you. You will probably overlook some conditions, and make assumptions about things you think the other party might want. The ideal mindset for this step is to wonder '*If I can do what I want, what would it look like?*' In other words, '*If I could wave a magic wand what would my ideal situation look like?*'

As long as you do not know what you wish to achieve, you will be under the influence of the other party, particularly if *they* are very clear on what they want. When unsure of what you want, you will also tend to consider the other party as an opponent, as a problem, because you will be reacting to their stated needs or wishes, often in a way that blocks progress.

Remember, your goal is clarified through the linkage tool (see Chapter 3).

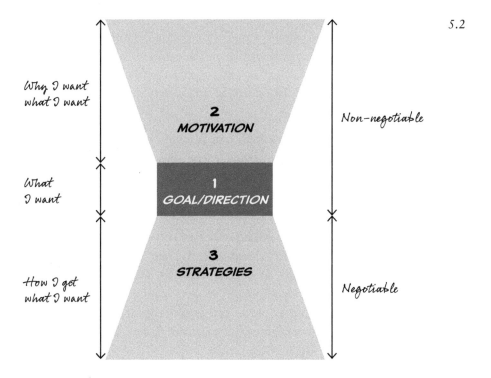

You are now in your **ego bubble** and can start defining your roadmap and its core elements:

- goal
- conditions
- ambitions
- limits
- questions
- information

These six elements make up your negotiation roadmap, which will be the basis for the encounter (step 3). You need to know clearly and hold true to what is negotiable and what is non-negotiable. A roadmap is a framework that clarifies your situation at this specific time in your life/project. Define it clearly and *believe in it*! The more you work on it, the clearer and more real it will become it your mind and hence the easier it will be to communicate. Here is how to build it.

How to set your goal

Your goal should always be written in the format '*I want*... (something) *under certain conditions.*'

This very simple formulation can be split into two distinct parts:

- *Part 1:* '*I want...*': This is what your goal really is, what you want to achieve, the end result. Nobody can stop you wanting what you want, although they can stop you getting it. The other party can stop you reaching your goal, but cannot stop you wanting it. This is the willingness, the volition prerequisite (see Chapter 3) – something that is non-negotiable, is not open for debate or modification. Your goal is non-negotiable.

- *Part 2:* '*... under certain conditions*': This is the indication that you are going to and are willing to negotiate, to enter into a bilateral process (rather than for instance to impose what you want). You do not want your goal under *any* conditions. You want it under *certain* conditions, which are what you are going to discuss with the other party. It is important to understand that you do not discuss your goal; you discuss the conditions under which you can reach it.

The rules for setting your goal are the following:

- A goal is non-negotiable.
- A goal must be inspiring, an opportunity, a driving force. The more your goal is inspiring, the greater your motivation to reach it, and the greater your resilience. Your self-confidence will also be impacted. Chapter 3 talks about the importance of motivation and resilience. Remember Locke and Lathan's conclusions to their research, that the way you set a goal is linked with higher motivation, self-esteem, self-confidence and autonomy.[4]
- A goal must always be positive and reflect an opportunity. A goal must never be formulated in a negative way: your subconscious doesn't hear negation, and it is incredibly difficult and counter-nature to fight to *not* achieve something. When faced with a negative aim (obviously there can be times when you do not wish for something), it is worth asking yourself '*What do I want instead of x?*' ('*If I don't want this situation, or if I could do what I wanted – what would that be?*'). This change of mindset will help you have a (slightly) different attitude and most likely in time help you actually look forward to trying to reach your goal. For instance – turn

around '*I do not want to work with X*' into '*I want to work with Y*', or '*I do not want to lose my job*' into '*I want to leave under the best possible conditions*'.

- You are always the subject of your subject. In other words, you must want something *for yourself*, you cannot want something for someone else. If you make the mistake of wanting something for someone else ('*I want you to do/be...*'), you are no longer in your ego bubble. The other becomes responsible for the achievement of your aim, and therefore the conditions you think about will be based on assumptions about them, what you think they might want, how you would react if they were to ask you X, what ploy can you use to bring them on board. You also waste precious time that would be more usefully spent thinking of your conditions. You should only think of yourself and what you want. '*I want something for me/my team/my project/my family/my company...*'

Your conditions

A condition is the smallest negotiable unit, the breakdown of your goal into a number of relevant and meaningful items. '*I want to buy this flat*' – what does buying this flat actually mean to you? It means thinking about elements such as the price, the moving-in date, any renovation work to be carried out, insurances, signing the contract date, cleaning it fully before you move in, whether or not the current furniture is to be changed, etc.

Conditions need to be very precise, plentiful and varied. For this, be creative (remember creativity is one of the prerequisites for a good negotiation). It is really important to have many conditions, in fact the more the better. A helpful idea when listing conditions is to sort them into families:

- Conditions to do with the **product/service/object**, for instance the actual product you want to buy (the microscope, the car, the house, the packaging you need for your shop) or services you are interested in (graphic designer, IT support) or the object to be negotiated (a treaty, a social contract).
- Conditions to do with the **relationship** you would like to have with the other party, for instance a supplier, another department, a neighbouring council. Such conditions could include whether you have a dedicated key account manager, how often the meetings will occur, what happens if there is a problem, what channels of communication will be used.

- Conditions pertaining to **contractual issues**. These are often the first ones to be thought of: the cost and pricing, the delivery, the quantity, the start date, the salary, the holiday allowance to name a few.

- Conditions to do with the **organization/company/institute**. For instance, if looking for a new employment or a research collaboration, do you prefer working for a start-up or an international organization? Where ideally would the company or university be located? Would it be small or medium size? For a partnership, is a national collaboration to be preferred over an international one?

This subdivision can help bring more clarity and creativity. Examples of conditions linked to specific situations will be found in the Appendix.

All conditions need to be very clearly defined, leaving no room for interpretation. All parties need to have the same definition for and understanding of a condition as they will be binding and will often figure in a contract or an agreement. It is particularly important to check understanding when dealing with people who do not share the same mastery of the language with which you are negotiating. The more conditions you have, the higher your

5.3   **HOW TO FORMULATE A GOAL**

I WANT X...   **... UNDER CERTAIN CONDITIONS**

What I want is non-negotiable

What is negotiable is the conditions under which I could obtain it

RULES FOR THE GOAL

1 *Not negotiable*
2 *I am the subject of my subject ~ I want something for me*
3 *Cannot be negative*
4 *Must be inspiring – something I really want*

incentive to be flexible, because it is only through flexibility that you will obtain new conditions. In other words, as will be seen in Chapter 10, you start your negotiation with the value of your ambition and, *under certain conditions*, you are willing to move away from it. You thus compensate for moving away from your ambition with a new condition.

Conditions cannot be negative or have a zero (i.e. '*I refuse this condition, I do not want it*') value as this would mean that you thought about the other party with a '*I will say no to their request.*' For instance, imagine a group leader or a HR manager making the assumption that a specific relocation package will be asked for and preparing to refuse it: '*If they asks for a relocation package I will say no.*'

This should be avoided for two reasons: first of all, it is in your interest to wait for the other to make the request and then to think about the conditions under which you might be willing to accept – because then you may negotiate something in return for agreeing in part or wholly to their request, following the dynamics of exchange. The second reason is

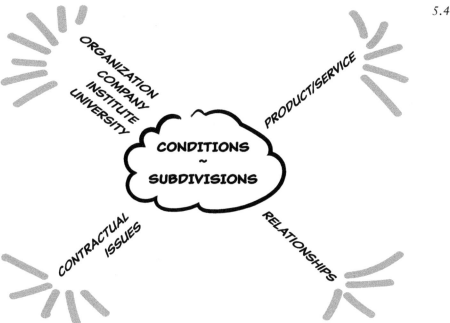

5.4

that preparation time is often scarce and it is in your best interest to focus on you and what you want rather than on a potential request (which might never even occur) from the other. This topic will be explored in Chapter 6.

> Remember at all times that what you do not think about you will not ask for, and what you do not ask for you probably will not get. So make sure you give yourself sufficient time to really think about and list all your conditions.

Setting boundaries on your conditions

A condition on its own is not useful; it is, in a way, simply a word, a label, something you can find in a dictionary. It needs boundaries. There are two possible boundaries: a positive one which in the five-step negotiation process is called an ambition, and a break-away one, called a limit.

The ambition: for every condition you define its ambition

An ambition represents the very best you wish to obtain on a condition. An ambition is not to be mistaken for an *acceptable* value, because acceptable implies *acceptable to the other party*. In building your roadmap, your ambition is truly a value to aim for, and can be calculated using a simple powerful formula. You decide what your condition is worth – your personal reference value (PRV). This PRV cannot be wrong, it is yours, based on your experience, your knowledge, your investigations.

You then decide what would be for you an ambitious or excellent deal, thus enhancing the estimated PRV figure. Thus you build your ambition, the value you will fight for. The equation is as follows:

You really believe in your ambition, that it is possible to reach it: the fact you believe in it is based on very careful preparation and homework. An ambition is never an unrealistic, fictitious, 'over the top' value.

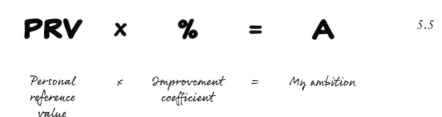

$$PRV \quad \times \quad \% \quad = \quad A \qquad 5.5$$

Personal reference value   ×   Improvement coefficient   =   My ambition

---

EXAMPLE

You want to sell your car. You check its reference price (PRV) using, in Switzerland for instance, the Swiss reference Argus price. This tells you how much your car is worth based on its number of kilometres, its age, the model, etc. Say its reference value for selling it is 2,700 francs. You then decide that for various reasons (such as you have never had an accident, you have regularly had it serviced, there are no scratch marks, etc) you want to sell it for a better price. You set your ambition for 3,200 francs which is what you will put in your advertisement. This is not in order to haggle, but to negotiate; under certain conditions you might be willing to accept less, but only under certain conditions.

An ambition is what drives you and your entire negotiation. It is your starting point and therefore it is one of the first things you communicate to the other party. You fight to achieve your ambition, you do not fight to defend your limits. Your impetus is trying to get what you want (to reach your goal) at the value of your ambitions. Every condition without exception has an ambition.

Your limits

Some conditions – and only some – have a limit. A limit is **the breaking point of any negotiation.** It is the point beyond which it is no longer in your interest to negotiate and you walk away, you stop the negotiation.

A limit:

- is carefully set and/or calculated
- is strong (you stick by it)
- is the one element of your roadmap that is kept totally secret
- is your breaking point

In reality, few conditions have a limit. Depending on the situation, approximately only 20 per cent of your conditions will have a limit, a breaking point. A limit must be strong and be respected (by you) – it is not an alibi to be used as a pressure lever.

One way of checking a limit is to imagine that you have obtained all you want at the value of your ambitions, except for the one condition whose limit you are testing. And you move, you change that limit (a token value, symbolic value +1/–1), and observe if you stand strong on your initial value. *For example, you want to move into your new flat on 30 June (your ambition), with a limit on 30 September.* Testing it, you play around with the date: *if the seller requests that you move in on 15 October, would you accept?* If yes, then your limit is weak. If you refuse and walk away, then your limit is strong. Bear in mind that if you are weak on one limit, the other party will perceive it and you will risk losing credibility on other stated values. A strong limit holds power.

Some conditions thus have a limit, the majority do not; in reality, real breaking points are often quite rare.

There is an important difference between conditions that have a limit and those that don't: a condition that has a limit is called a **vital** condition, i.e. if it does not figure in an agreement, the agreement cannot happen – it is vital to the deal. A vital condition is thus recognized by the fact that it has a limit. The more vital conditions you have, the harder your negotiation will be as each one is a potential breaking point, and therefore you react differently when talking about and dealing with them, generally being less flexible.

All other conditions are optional or 'champagne' conditions (i.e. additional ones) and make up the bulk of your conditions. These differ from vital conditions in that they do not have a limit, but are nevertheless good, interesting, useful, nice to have, at times a real bonus. They can be very important – in fact at times more so than a vital condition, with the difference being that if they are not part of the agreement, the agreement can still be signed. The reason why they can be called 'champagne' is that although they can at times be valuable and important, they hold no potential to break a deal. For instance, imagine you have been offered the ideal job, the one you have dreamt of for many years, that is located in the centre of a big city. The downside is that you live in a remote location with little access to public transport, hence you rely on your car for transport. One of the conditions you will try to negotiate is a parking place in the company's parking lot. This will not be vital in that if they do not agree you will not refuse the job (you might have to move, find a room during the week, or organize car sharing), but it definitely is a 'champagne' condition that is very valuable to you.

Information

The last two elements to be filled in your roadmap relate to information. What was prepared during the contextual analysis (Chapter 4) pertaining to information will be added on your roadmap, because it will ensure it is not forgotten during the encounters, your roadmap being your main supporting tool when you are negotiating. Information plays a crucial role in any negotiation, be it information you share or you seek.

INFORMATION SHARING

Based on what was prepared during the contextual analysis, you fill in this part of your roadmap with the elements you believe are in your interest that the other knows about you, the situation, your project, your organization. Think strategically as this will help create interest and usually influences your counterpart. Make sure you are dealing with facts and not opinions.

GOAL: *I WANT TO SELL MY CAR UNDER CERTAIN CONDITIONS*   *5.6*

CONDITIONS	AMBITIONS	LIMITS
CAR PRICE	3200 francs	₤2500 francs*
DEPOSIT	100%	60%
PAYMENT CONDITIONS	Cash	
DELIVERY/REMOVAL	They pick up	
DATE	Before XX/XX/XX	
CONTRACT	Signed ASAP	
CHANGE OF OWNERSHIP	Buyer	
BUYER	Local garage	

*Indicates I am willing to go lower than the market value

5.7

Roadmap

My goal

My ambitions   My conditions   My limit

A.
B.
C.
D.
E.
F.
G.
H.
J.
K.
L.
M.
N.
O.
...

QUESTIONS TO BE ASKED

Based on your contextual analysis, what are your questions? What do you need to know that you weren't able to find out alone? Rather than making hypotheses or assumptions, with the risk of being wrong, prepare questions and remember to ask them. A question relates to something you need to find out, a condition to something you would like to obtain.

Chapter 5: summary points

- Being very clear about your goal is fundamental to the success of your negotiation.
- When preparing your roadmap make sure you remain in your ego bubble and do not think about the other party.
- Develop an inspiring and positively stated goal, one you really want to achieve.
- Remember you do not negotiate your goal, you negotiate the conditions under which you can reach it.
- Drill down your goal into as many possible conditions as you can. Be creative, think outside of the box, unconventionally, be curious and inquisitive about possibilities, imagine all that would be really good to have that is coherent with your goal, how you would like your ideal deal to look. Do not only focus on what is strictly necessary.
- State an ambition that you believe in for each condition. This value will be the starting point of your negotiation, the value, what you will communicate to the other party and that you aim to achieve.
- Place a limit on any condition when you know that you cannot or will not go beyond this limit value. This limit signifies the breaking point of your negotiation, the point beyond which you no longer wish to or you no longer can negotiate and you pull out. A limit is strong and is the one element that is never shared with the other party.
- You fight to get as close as possible to your ambitions. You do not fight to defend your limits.
- Vital conditions are ones that have an ambition and a limit. Optional 'champagne' conditions only have an ambition. There are usually very few vital conditions (potential deal-breakers).

- Prepare questions to be asked about what you need to find out that you couldn't find out alone. Avoid imagining answers and making assumptions.

- List the information that is in your interest to share because it is relevant to the process and because you believe it will have a positive influence on the parties to stay engaged in the negotiations.

- Determine a roadmap that you will use as a framework throughout the encounters.

Notes

1   More details on this example can be found in the Appendix
2   N Mandela. 12 wise Nelson Mandela quotes that will inspire your success, *Inc.*, 2018. www.inc.com/peter-economy/17-wise-nelson-mandela-quotes-that-will-inspire-your-success.html (archived at https://perma.cc/2XZW-N3AZ)
3   J Goldstein (2013) *Mindfulness*, Sounds True, Louisville, CO
4   M R Chowdhury. The science and psychology of goal-setting 101, *Positive Psychology*, 2020. https://positivepsychology.com/goal-setting-psychology/ (archived at https://perma.cc/RW8W-7HJX)

PART THREE

Encounters and communication

The two main skills to be an excellent negotiator – one who clinches lasting deals and is respected in the process – are to be extremely well prepared, as discussed in Chapter 5, and to have excellent communication and listening skills. The following four chapters focus on the importance of communication for successful negotiations. Chapter 6 introduces the encounter and its structure; Chapter 7 explores communication tools necessary for good negotiations to happen, building a concrete simple toolbox; Chapter 8 focuses on online negotiations and Chapter 9 on non-cognitive elements to take into account and use when meeting with the other parties.

06

Step 3: the encounters

This chapter focuses on meeting the other party and communication. Once you know what you want, you will need to understand how to communicate it in order to reach your goal, or at least get closer to it. When negotiating, it is not enough for one party alone (you) to get what you want: the bilaterality of the process requires that you also know what your counterparts and interlocutors want. Everyone needs to have their interest – at least in part – fulfilled to ensure each party's engagement in the agreed result. However fantastic you might be at selling your idea or project, if you do not get the others on board and also respond to their needs, your agreement will be one-sided with the high risk that what was agreed will not be put into place.

The mindset with which you meet the other will influence how you behave and communicate. In this chapter you will be reminded of the specific mindset necessary for a good encounter before learning about the necessary prerequisites for a good and useful meeting to happen. The structure of the negotiation encounter will be outlined, together with its three distinct parts: the introduction, the core and the closure. Some examples will enable you to better understand the relationship between the opening statement that will be given during the introduction and the linkage tool.

From building trust and rapport, to following one's roadmap and letting it be known what you want, and finally to understanding what the other party wants and needs: the purposes of the encounter are numerous.

Encounter context and prerequisites

The encounter is the moment when you meet the other party, whether face-to-face or virtually. To put the encounter back into context, there are three pillars to excellence in negotiating partnerships and agreements:

- the mindset – considering the other party as your opportunity
- excellent preparation
- very strong listening skills

The mindset

As explained in Chapter 1, your **mindset** is fundamental throughout the process, because the way you consider the other party is going to influence your attitude, your communication style, your verbal and non-verbal language, your patience and resilience, as well as your assumptions and the way you interpret what they say and how they behave. In fact, your mindset will influence the entire process. Because you require the other party to reach your goal, the first thing you should do is therefore to make sure that you fundamentally consider them an opportunity, realizing they are someone you need (because it would be harder or impossible to achieve your result alone).

Excellent preparation

You need to know exactly what you want, i.e. your **roadmap** must be clear in your mind. This will enable you to be totally focused on the other party, in an interested, concentrated and not pushy way.

Being well prepared and knowing exactly what you want is of primary importance: if you are not clear in your own mind about what you want to achieve, you will not only be under the influence of the other, but will have the added challenge to get your message across clearly. The clearer your goal, the easier it is to express it so that it is understood in an unambiguous way.

Strong listening skills

An excellent negotiator is characterized by excellent **listening skills.**

Why listen rather than seek to convince the other? Some people excel with the spoken word, are great at influencing and convincing in a compelling way, taking over the conversation, and in the process they often leave little room for the other and their (at times different) opinions. These people forget a fundamental aspect – they forget or ignore that the solutions will almost invariably come from what the other party says, *because the other party knows what they need to engage in the process.*

To negotiate an agreement or deal that will be honoured, you need your counterparts' buy-in – because by definition a negotiation is a bi- or multi-lateral exercise. So you must find out what they want and what they need, you will question them if the information is not readily available, and you will seek to establish a good rapport if they are withdrawn, wary or shy, i.e. *you need to engage and you need them to engage.* You will also need to voice the content of your roadmap, and express your own needs, wishes and concerns in an open and cooperative way.

In complex negotiations, for instance with various teams involved in a project and where all the participants are needed to make the project move forward, the best way to engage everyone involves a considerable amount of finding out and listening with all the stakeholders. The more that people are allowed to contribute and participate, the more they will feel committed to the negotiated agreement, to the end result. This is important because the commitment of all parties is definitely needed to put the agreement into effect.

Jennifer Potenta, a director in MetLife's Corporate Private Placements group, said, 'Listening is really important because sometimes you *think* you know what the other party wants, but when you listen, you really *hear* what they want. That's where you get to a position, a resolution, that works for both sides.'[1]

On communication and transparency

'When you want to fool the world, tell the truth.'[2] Otto von Bismarck's famous quote highlights an – at times – surprising fact. Transparency can have a disarming effect in a world where many transactions are based on hidden agendas, manipulative tactics and information retention, as well as hopes and expectations that the other has understood a message you haven't managed to say. Frustrating, lengthy, at times sterile conversations can lead to at best a waste of time, and at worst severe misunderstandings, giving rise to unpleasant or even conflictual situations. Family and work environments are rife with such examples. People often make assumptions that the other person knows what they want. They are then surprised when the other person does not react as hoped and can even at times take offence. Always remember:

If I don't know what you want I can't help you get it, and if you don't know what I want you can't help me get it.

A rule of thumb is that if you do not talk about or ask for something you most probably will not get it.

You will share information, using your roadmap as a starting point, bringing into the conversation your conditions with their ambitions (remember: your limits are never to be mentioned) in such a way as to be clear that they are negotiable (when they are), that you are open and curious, that this is 'only' a (first) discussion, a starting point. No commitments will be made during the encounters. The fact that no commitments or promises are made during the encounters lowers the pressure and increases the feeling of 'emotional' safety. The proper attitude is to be relaxed, open and cooperative, and at the same time highly focused and concentrated.

No commitment on a condition is ever made during an encounter. Conditions are only discussed and agreed upon hypothetically. You are not clinching a deal, but walking gradually step-by-step towards a possible agreement.

The aim of an encounter and how it actually works

The aim of an encounter (and remember there may be – and usually are – several encounters as negotiation is an iterative process) is threefold:

- to say what you want, to tell your counterpart your goal and conditions
- to find out what your counterpart wants, needs, what is of value to them, what the context is, to understand them, what they may be worried about, what issues they need to tackle, what their interest may be
- to potentially discover new conditions

During the encounter, you are in fact trying to map the other party's road-map: their goal, their conditions, their ambitions, their limits: like a consultant who is working with a customer to define – and at times help them define when they don't know – what they really want.

Interestingly enough, as many people tend to 'think for others', one of the consequences of the encounter is the discovery of new items that can be turned into conditions for oneself. Discussions and curiosity breed creativity and opportunity. Multicultural encounters are particularly interesting for discovering new possibilities, because people from different backgrounds and cultures see things differently.

Structure

The structure of an encounter is as follows:

- the introduction:
  - ○ welcome
  - ○ presentations

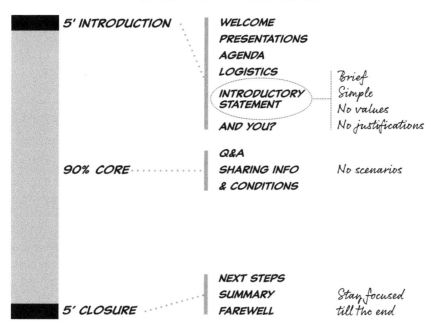

STRUCTURE OF AN ENCOUNTER   6.2

5' INTRODUCTION
WELCOME
PRESENTATIONS
AGENDA
LOGISTICS — Brief
INTRODUCTORY STATEMENT — Simple / No values / No justifications
AND YOU?

90% CORE
Q&A
SHARING INFO & CONDITIONS — No scenarios

5' CLOSURE
NEXT STEPS
SUMMARY
FAREWELL — Stay focused till the end

- agenda
- logistics
- introductory statement
- opening to the other
- the core:
  - questions and answers
  - information sharing
- the closure:
  - next steps
  - summary
  - farewell

The introduction (five minutes)

Two crucial and strategic[3] moments in a meeting are at the beginning (to create safety) and at the end (to clarify next steps and decisions). The aim of the introduction (which is very brief) is primarily to create a constructive and safe atmosphere, as free as possible from shadow areas (i.e. items that have not been discussed, questions that aren't asked, worries people may have, feelings there may be hidden agendas, etc). People need to feel safe to talk openly; a secure environment is required. Creating such an environment is important – and can start as early as when you plan the location and calendar (see contextual analysis in Chapter 4).

WELCOME
It is important to set the scene and to welcome the participants, being careful to respect cultural customs. An error or clumsiness at this stage can damage the relationship or at best simply create some unease.

PRESENTATIONS
Here all the parties present themselves. Who are you, what do *you* want your counterpart to know about you? What is it *in your interest* that they know? (You may wish to refer back the contextual analysis and to the information section of your roadmap.) Remember that everything you say about yourself will influence how you are perceived. Obviously your words alone are not the only thing that matter and influence, but they count and this is

strategic to remember. So be clear on what you want to say (do you want to mention your title, your function, your seniority and years in the organization, your personal situation, your nationality, activities you are involved in as a volunteer?). Also, if you are with a team, remember to present all members, introducing their functions and the role they will play during the negotiations. Obviously you will avoid saying '*I am pilot and X is co-pilot*' and say instead '*I will be leading this meeting and my colleague Joe will be taking notes, and be our time keeper*'.

AGENDA

This is the point where you clarify the length of the meeting and make it clear that there may be several encounters. Knowing that all does not need to be concluded within one session often lowers pressure. Good time-keeping is always necessary, even more so if the situation is complex and challenging. If the encounter is going to last more than one hour, plan a short break and make sure the participants are informed.

LOGISTICS

Is there anything your guests need to know to feel more comfortable? Is there anything you need for the meeting to run smoothly, such as equipment, electronics, a paper board, specific rules (see also Chapter 8 on online negotiations)? For meetings where participants are physically present you might want to think about the seating arrangements and the shape and positioning of the table, if you have one, and the chairs. Who sits next to whom can, for instance, show you have found out and care to respect various cultural behaviours and norms. Logistic aspects relevant to online sessions will be discussed in Chapter 8 on online negotiations.

INTRODUCTORY STATEMENT

This is where you tell the other party what your goal is, what you *would like* to achieve with these negotiations, what the meeting is about. Simply put, you refer back to your written goal (on your roadmap) in a specific open format, i.e. preferring words such as '*I would like*' to '*I want*'. You state clearly what you would like to reach or get (remember your goal is non negotiable: you are not there to discuss your goal, you are there to discuss the conditions under which you can achieve it) and then you listen to the other's reaction. Ultimately you are seeking to understand what it would take for them to give you what you are asking for. What is important is to show you are strong and clear on your goal, and open and flexible on the conditions. The more inspired and clear you are about your goal, the easier it will be to communicate it.

EXAMPLES

'I would like to work with your organization, and am here today to discuss the conditions under which I could be part of your supplier team...'

'We would like to bring food and medicine to the refugee camp over the river, and we are here to discuss what we can do to count on your support in this task...'

'I need your team's support on this project and would like to talk about the possibilities for us coming to an agreement on resource allocation...'

'I need to make sure some security is set on our database, and would like to know what I can do to make sure this is done...'

6.3

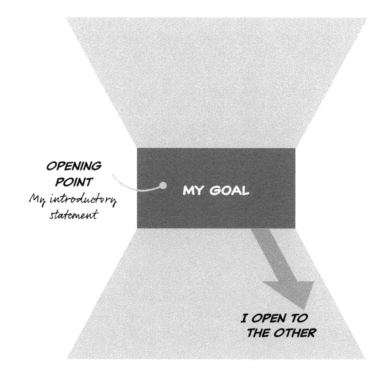

OPENING POINT
My introductory statement

MY GOAL

I OPEN TO THE OTHER

As in Figure 6.3, the opening point is the point beyond which the other party has something to add, to say, to be involved in. You might wish to say something about why you want what you want, although this is not always even necessary or a good idea (see Chapter 3).

Some rules for the introductory statement:

- In the opening statement you give no values, nothing that could provoke a negative reaction or in fact any (strong) reaction. In other words there is nothing negotiable in your opening statement.

- Stay brief, straightforward, non-ambiguous and simple. Prefer fewer words to more.

- Do not justify anything. However, *if it is in your interest*, you can give one reason why you want what you want (in Figure 6.3 this will be in the top of the linkage funnel).

EXAMPLES

'In order to promote bioinformatics for research on eradicating malaria, I would like to set up a partnership with your foundation and would like to discuss the conditions that would lead you to accept us as a partner.'

'In order to ensure a peaceful transition to outsourcing our IT facilities, we would like to have a clear agreement as to how we are to proceed with closing our data centre, and would like to talk with you about how we can come to this agreement.'

If you are doing the introduction, once you have put your point of view across, then open to the other party: '*And you?*' You then indicate to the other party that the discussion is open, and that you are now happy to listen to them, to what they want out of this meeting (hoping they actually know it).

The core 90 per cent

The main part of the meeting takes place in what is called the core. In fact, 90 per cent of the encounter takes place in this section, with questions, answers, information sharing.

The first – and very challenging – rule during the core of the meeting is '**no scenario**': indeed you should not build and work on a scenario for the simple reason that you do not know how your counterpart is going to react to what you say and how they will answer your questions. If you have prepared a possible scenario for the conversation, you will tend to interpret everything the other person says in such a way as to make it fit into your assumptions, even in an unconscious way. Your listening will be directed and biased, your filters strong, and your questions may even become manipulative.

Your roadmap is the thread of the encounter, and information sharing will take an open flow format, with your goal, conditions and ambitions always in mind. Once you have told the other party what you want, you then seek conversational opportunities to bring in your conditions, clearly stating your ambitions. Remember – if the other party does not know what you want, it will be difficult for them to help you get it. It is always more strategic to start from your ambitions and fix the conditions under which you are willing to move away from them than to talk about your limits and try to 'climb back up the steep hill' towards your ambitions. Your roadmap in mind, you talk about your conditions when it is fit, bundling them when appropriate. You do not bring in your conditions as a 'shopping list' except if specifically asked, as in, for instance: '*What do you need in order to set up a lab?*' Or '*What do you need to run your workshop in our hotel?*' (see below for a detailed example). Only when specifically asked should you bring in your list of best requirements.

EXAMPLE

A company wants to organize a workshop. They ask you: '*Please let us know what the various requirements are for your workshop logistics.*' You answer with your list of ideal conditions for the location and logistics: '*What would be ideal is to have a large room with desks and chairs in a U shape, two flip charts, water for each participant, name holders, and a break-out room with one table and six chairs…*'.

This could be represented in a roadmap format as:

TABLE 6.1

Conditions	Ambitions	Limits
Room	One large room with windows that can be opened	
Seating	One desk per participant with chairs in a U shape	No U possible
Beverage	Water (fizzy and still) and glasses for trainer and participants changed daily	
Material	Pad and pencil for each participant	
	Name holders	
	2 flip charts on wheels with coloured felt pens	
	Tape	
	A pin board	
Break-out room	With table and 6 chairs, very close to the main room	
Tables	One for the trainer with 2 chairs	
Breaks	Coffee, tea, orange juice and biscuits in a separate room/location	
...		

So when your interlocutor asks you what you want, you make the most of this opportunity, being careful not to say you *want*, but '*what you would like*', or '*the best would be*' or '*ideally it would look like this*' – which indicates a degree of flexibility. Make sure you are constantly aware of your counterpart's reaction: do not wear blinkers, at all times remain alert and observant.

If your counterpart does not ask specifically for your conditions, you bring them into the discussion when it seems the best moment to, making sure you get or ask for the other's (initial) reaction. If you communicate your ambitions and get no reaction, you have no idea if there is a possibility that they will say *yes*, or *maybe*, or if it is a clear *no*. At some point you will definitely need a reaction to what you have asked for. So leave time for the other to respond, always bearing in mind that different people have different speeds of reaction and ways of responding. Being aware of different personality traits, such as the different ways introverts and extroverts process data and react, will be extremely helpful:[4] some people need more time to process information and to respond than others. For instance, a common mistake is to interpret silence as agreement or boredom. If you need an answer, then you may need to insist, politely, or agree to a date when you can have an answer if this is not during the meeting. This point is particularly relevant when engaged in an online meeting (see Chapter 8).

You need to make sure that at least your most important conditions are talked about as well as your vital ones. Not all conditions are mentioned – usually there are far too many (remember the flexibility and strength of your negotiation lies in the quantity and attractiveness (to you) of your conditions) but make sure you talk about the ones you most wish to see in the agreement or contract as well as all the vital ones. Maybe 60–70 per cent of all your conditions will be mentioned in the final deal.

If you are accompanied by one or several people, remember to have agreed before the encounter who will lead it (pilot) and who will take notes (co-pilot), and on how you switch roles if needed. The tool in Chapter 7 can be used to take notes so that they are structured and you can refer back to them when required.

The closure (five to ten minutes)

It is important to end a meeting in a specific and careful way, in order not to leave loose ends. Make sure the next steps are clear, summarize, write down all the items discussed and if and when a next meeting was arranged.

Increased involvement of all parties brings the benefit of increased commitment (which is fundamental to the partnership being put into action, even if it may take longer to reach). The less that people are or feel involved, the less they commit to the final decision. This is most important when everybody *must* support the final choice. The clearer the picture, the less likely people are to be disappointed, or unpleasantly surprised.

How to respond when someone specifically enquires about your limit

It can happen that the other party asks you what your limit is (e.g. '*How far can you go?*', '*What is your budget?*', '*What is your final price?*'). Avoid giving a straight answer and telling them what your limit is; always come back to what you ideally hoped for. Remember, if you communicate your limit, you may be sure that you will never get even close to your ambition.

If the other party gives you a value that is beyond your limit, simply respond with '*I am afraid that is not possible... supposing we could be flexible on X would you agree to Y?*'

Can a limit be changed?

In some situations, after one or more encounters, when analysing the conditions that have been discussed and possibly new conditions that have cropped up, you may realize that it actually is possible for you to change a limit. *On no account should you change a limit in front of the other party.* Make sure you are with your team, far from anyone else, and analyse your roadmap and note taking to make sure that you do not lose out by moving a limit, and that you compensate accordingly whatever movement you make.

The next chapter will take you through some useful tools and recommendations to ensure your encounters are foundations on which to get closer to an agreement.

Chapter 6: summary points

- Excellent negotiators have highly developed listening skills and build on their capacity to fully understand their counterparts to make a difference and stand out.
- Strong listening skills are conducive to building trust and creating a rapport. Both are necessary for an agreement to be effectively put into practice and for encouraging the parties towards action.
- Encounters follow a structure, but never a scenario – you never know where your counterpart is going to take you. If you have a carefully built mental scenario your focus will be less on what the other party is really saying but more on how they could fit into your pre-prepared scenario.
- The clearer your goal is in your mind, the easier it is to communicate.
- When taking part in an encounter, make sure you are vigilant, well rested and fully concentrated. At all times, show your interest in your counterparts whilst never forgetting your aim. Always keep your roadmap present in the back of your mind.

- Encounters are not about convincing others and winning an argument. Encounters are about finding the conditions under which you will be able to strike a deal.
- Interest remains crucial until the end – if any one party loses interest, they will not engage. This applies for all the parties involved, including you.
- Remember at all times: '*If I don't know what you want I can't help you get it, and if you don't know what I want you can't help me get it.*'

Notes

1 Knowledge@Wharton. Women and negotiation: Are there really gender differences? 2015. https://knowledge.wharton.upenn.edu/article/women-and-negotiation-are-there-really-gender-differences (archived at https://perma.cc/H469-LQ9B)
2 O von Bismarck. www.goodreads.com/quotes/169528-when-you-want-to-fool-the-world-tell-the-truth (archived at https://perma.cc/5QZ2-VH6H)
3 K Patterson, A Switzler, J Grenny and R McMillan (2012) *Crucial Conversations: Tools for talking when stakes are high*, McGraw-Hill, New York
4 M Laney (2002) *The Introvert Advantage: How to thrive in an extrovert world*, Workman Publishing Company, New York

07

Tools for use during encounters

In this chapter you will learn how to talk about your roadmap, once it is developed, whilst at the same time finding out what your counterpart wants and needs and what their position is. The way you present your roadmap will have a great impact on how it is received and understood, ensuring that your communication style and language reflect the fact that you are fully engaged in a bilateral process, i.e. that you are negotiating and not imposing.

The first part shares some insight on how to communicate your roadmap. Then you will be presented with a number of simple and straightforward yet powerful communication tools and listening skills to help you during your encounters. Next, a brief overview of useful attitudes to have when communicating will be presented, with a focus on some aspects of non-violent communication that are especially relevant when negotiating. These considerations will help you to understand some factors that influence good interpersonal communication: knowing how to communicate will play a vital role in your success as a negotiator. Finally, the topics of body language, non-verbal and para-verbal communication will be explored because they have a strong impact on how messages are conveyed and on how each party is perceived. Trust breeds through non-verbal communication and needs to be built for lasting negotiations to happen. The chapter ends with a list of recommendations and summary points to keep in mind when facing the other party.

More on communicating your roadmap

You as an individual do not decide what a message means and how it is understood; *the receiver of the message* decides that. It is never possible to control all the reactions, feelings or thoughts that a message may trigger in the receiver. It is, however, advisable to be aware of and sensitive to them and how they may differ from your intent, and to *acknowledge* those reactions.

During the encounter, when talking, start with small issues, preferably easy ones, and use tentative language, separating intent from outcome. Avoid nagging or insisting on a point, and try never to lose hope or revert to aggressive behaviour or words; it is important at all times – however frustrated you might feel – to stay open and cooperative, ensuring you maintain a feeling of safety, always remembering that to discuss and explore does not mean to commit.

When talking with those holding opposing opinions, the more convinced and forceful you are, the more resistant they will become, whereas the more tentatively you speak, the more open people become to your suggestions.

Never use threats and accusations, as it kills safety. Translate silence and aggressive signals as signs that people are feeling unsafe and do something to restore a feeling of safety, such as for instance being curious (asking questions) and being patient (not pushing). In other words, as common wisdom goes, *don't get furious – get curious*; have in mind at all times that you listen to understand, not to react.

Stay focused and strong when it comes to knowing what you want, avoiding 'either/or' choices, which tend to deter creativity. The easiest and most straightforward way to encourage others to speak is to invite them to express themselves by showing genuine interest, which is helped by the fact that you realize you need them and they are an opportunity for you. So in fact, your interest *is* genuine.

Whenever the other party mentions a figure that is far from your ambition on a condition you need to make sure that the fact is mentioned in a calm way.

EXAMPLE

Consider a discussion concerning the price of a table. Both buyer and seller will have 'price' as a condition.

TABLE 7.1

Conditions	Ambition	Limit
Buyer price	£300	£450
Seller price	£500	£250

If the buyer (B) says '*I would like to buy the table you are selling and am willing to pay £300*', the seller (S) should respond with something like '*I am glad you are interested, however I had a higher figure in mind. I actually was hoping for £500.*' Note the past tense, which indicates that S is willing to move. Then B could continue with a hypothetical question:

B: '*What if we were to pay cash and pick it up today, would you be willing to sell it for £300?*'

B is thus indicating that B believes in and is 'fighting' for their ambition, and at the same time suggesting two new conditions (cash and picking up), checking openly that S might be interested in them, therefore hoping to create interest for S to move and accept the offered price.

As mentioned in the previous chapter, your aim is to share your goal and conditions at the value of your ambitions and to focus on your counterparts' potential conditions, finding out about the ones you might fulfil (in exchange for something you desire). You might even be lucky if some of their conditions come at a low cost for you but have high value for them. For instance, an independent graphic designer might have the high value condition of being able to use, for marketing purposes, a well-known customer's logo on their website, thus indicating that they have worked for this important customer. This condition might be of little value to the customer and easy to accept.

The negotiator–communicator toolbox

Some communication tools will help you enhance the usefulness and flow of your encounters and help you negotiate better. Remember to use these tools with your personal touch and creativity, with your own language and communication style, and vary your usage of the tools in the list below. The general flow should always be open and cooperative, as you are not pushing for an agreement and firm commitment but advancing step-by-step towards a possible deal. Always look for the need and interest of the other party, and keep in mind that listening does not mean accepting!

Questions

Several types of questions exist:

- *Open:* To invite the other to talk more and share more information.
  - *What does integrity of research mean for you?*
  - *How would you like your project to be run?*
  - *How do you think the department should be organized?*
- *Closed:* To provide a short validation answer.
  - *Do you need an overhead projector?*
  - *Do you have a laptop?*
- *Echo:* To prompt further description, repeating the last word someone has said, and echoing it, using your voice to prompt for clarification – voice rises slightly.
  - A says: '*I am working on a new USB stick.*' B answers with an echo: '*USB stick?*'

o A replies: '*Yes, one of those technical…*'

- *Hypothetical:* To test what would happen if an agreement on a specific condition was met, to make a hypothesis towards a potential positive outcome if…

  o '*Supposing we manage to agree on a price – could the sale take place by the end of August?*'

  o '*If we succeeded in getting approval by the end of June, would you be able to deliver by the end of August?*'

  o '*Imagine we have the budget we want for this conference, would you be willing to be our keynote speaker?*'

- *'Sending back':* When the other talks about what they don't want or is not being clear on their needs, help them to engage into a problem solving or a solution focused attitude.

  o '*What do you want (from me, from the situation)? How can I help? How would you like it to be/change?*'

  o '*What do you need?*'

  o '*If you do not wish for this, what would you want instead?*'

Listening skills

To paraphrase Goethe, talking is a necessity in life but listening is an art. Excellent listening skills are fundamental in negotiations as they enable you to understand what your counterpart says and means (which are not always the same), and will help you be attentive to what they don't say. Listening to the spoken word, the reaction, the unspoken message will all help you to understand what will influence the other party to engage in a negotiation with you. Most people listen to react rather than listen to understand, because they are mainly concerned with what they plan to reply. In other words their focus is most often geared towards themselves. Good listening provokes good storytelling because showing interest invites people to talk to you. Strong listening skills are what you need in order to invite your counterpart to share what is important to them, what they value, what the issues are that mean the most.

There are five golden rules to being and showing you are a good listener:

1 *Do not multitask* (i.e. no phones, messages, chats or emails when you are engaged in a conversation with someone). The only other thing you can do is take notes.

2 *Be curious and show it.* Make sure the other party realizes you are listening to them and that they have your entire attention.

3 *Stay focused and concentrated.* Often it is the non-verbal language or the 'little words' that someone says that will give away interesting information worth asking about.

4 *Listen to understand,* not to respond and counter-argue.

5 *Remember at all times that you need your counterpart* and this dialogue is the most important means for you to know them and what they want.

Active listening

Good communication requires feedback and response – and feedback can take the form of active listening. Active listening is first and foremost an attitude, one that aims to ensure the other party feels they are being listened to. There are many ways to show this, and it was once mentioned to me: '*If you really are listening, there is nothing more to do.*'

To demonstrate active listening:

- Concentrate. Show that you are attentive (appreciative words, nods, body language, etc).
- Reformulate, check understanding, summarize.
- Express your interest, be curious, ask questions, using all the tools in this section.
- Be sincere and genuine.
- Use your body language to show presence. However, be careful with eye contact and physical proximity. Eye contact in many cultures (and interestingly enough in the animal kingdom) is often a sign of threat or defiance. It is very important to be clear on the cultural norms of the people with whom you are talking.

Acknowledging

Helpful to active listening, acknowledging provides feedback and response to communication.

'*You really sound upset and hurt...*'

'*I see that you are angry about...*'

Acknowledging does not mean agreeing. It means making sure the other feels that they have been heard and that their reaction or emotion has not dismissed. Often, being acknowledged is a strong step towards defusing aggression. Someone who repeats themselves is someone who does not feel they have been heard or listened to. Try this with a child when they come home in tears from school – just acknowledging their sadness without directly offering a comment first.

Rephrasing and reformulating

Paraphrasing what the other party has said is an excellent way a) to show they have been listened to and b) to check that you have understood what they said, which can lead to correction or clarification.

Paraphrase and reformulate in an abbreviated way, using your or their words:

'If I understand correctly, the technology used to make the presentation is very important for you and the message you want to get across is...'

'So what you are trying to say is you would like our after-sales service to be delivered in an automated way within 24 hours.'

Silence

Silence is such a powerful and ambiguous tool!

There are so many possible interpretations to be made when someone falls silent, and often interpretations fall short of reality. When your counterpart is being silent, are they thinking? Analysing what you have just said? Bored? Planning their answer? Daydreaming? Pausing? Too upset to speak? And if silence occurs during a virtual meeting, is it the technology or the sign of some displeasure?[1]

When *you* are silent, you are not giving justifications, not arguing your point, not trying to convince, not saying something you might regret. Your silence can speak louder than words. Furthermore, when you are silent you are giving space to the other party, inviting them to fill in that space, even giving yourself time to think. Only when you are silent can you listen and invite the other to talk.

Silence is an incredibly powerful means of inviting someone to speak, and must be accompanied by coherent facial and eye expression (i.e. attentive, not bored, smiling, not aggressive). It is not always easy being comfortable with silence though. Practise using fewer words and leaving moments of silence (even as little as a regular three-second silence) during a dialogue. People who talk too much can give away information they would have preferred to keep to themselves. Another point to bear in mind is that silence is used differently depending on personality. For instance, an introvert will tend to spend more time thinking in silence than a more extrovert person, who will often 'think out loud'.[2]

Tools for the co-pilot

The following four tools are specifically used by the **co-pilot**, if you have one, although if negotiating alone you will still use them.

Reframing

It can happen that the conversation veers away from the main topic. Reframing will remind those present what the meeting is about and politely invite people to return to the main subject.

Taking notes

Taking notes is important and a prerequisite for the next step, which is the offer, as the notes will have captured the essence of the discussion, each party's position, various facts and values, etc. This is another important task for the co-pilot. Notes must be factual, useful, clear and efficient. The notes that have been taken will be used to make summaries and, often, to build an offer. Taking notes in fact is similar to trying to re-construct the roadmap of the other party. Always remember to check when a value is given, and if it is not what you hoped for (i.e. not your ambition) check to see if it is negotiable.

The following tool will assist you in your note taking.

Summarizing

A summary is incredibly useful for several reasons, such as to:

- check understanding and give space to the other to correct or complete
- slow the rhythm and give time to think

TABLE 7.2

Their aim

Their conditions	Their value + *(possibly their A)*	Their value − *(possibly their L)*	My reaction My comments

Their questions

Other comments

- take control of a conversation that has been hijacked (in case of anger or emotional overflow, for instance) in a polite way
- offer security anchors: when you end the meeting and fix another date to continue, you do not start from scratch
- reframe the discussion

Summaries always happen before ending an encounter and therefore before making an offer (see Chapter 10).

A summary should be made in a 'bullet point' style, i.e. with no extra words, no opinions, definitely not listing the various arguments or justifications that have been given, nothing more that the bare facts and what has been said. Imagine you need to send an email and you must pay a considerable amount of money for every word you type: you would choose very carefully what you write. Use a few useful words. A summary is neutral, therefore it can be made by any one party and cover all that has been said (by you, by them). The others can – if needed – complete it or correct it. A summary is usually made by reading one's notes and thus helps ensure they are correct and complete. An encounter may have short summaries every 15 minutes. Always keep in mind that what has not been summarized is probably not written down in the notes, and therefore will most likely be forgotten in the final agreement. As mentioned, if there is a co-pilot they will make the summary; if not, then it is up to you as pilot to do it.

Suggesting a break

When and why is it important to take a break? Breaks must be frequent and regular, taken on request or when the need is felt, for instance in case of tiredness, boredom, need to clarify ideas, discuss in private, seek additional information, check data, review one's strategy, elaborate an offer. If you notice that your counterpart is tired or looking bored, you can take the initiative of suggesting a break. Once more, usually, this task belongs to the co-pilot if you have one, but anyone can ask for a break if they deem it necessary.

Be aware of the signals and do not attempt to 'push' and continue the discussion when your counterpart is obviously tired, bored or not concentrating. This is especially relevant when the meetings are run online (see Chapter 8). When taking a break, it is important to change location and remain discreet, making sure no private documents are left behind. A lot can be learned from flip charts, scrap papers, roadmaps that have their limits clearly visible.

Other things to bear in mind

What follows are some recommendations that will prove useful during the encounters.

Beware of assumptions

Assumptions and judgements are widespread and potential dynamite: it is rare to listen without 'translating' the information you are receiving based on your own assumptions and filters. At times it can be so easy to assume you 'just know' what they mean or feel, jump ahead and finish the other person's sentence for them, or prepare your next question or answer before they have even finished speaking, and the actual meaning of what they are saying is lost or misunderstood. Always question your assumptions.

Work on facts and accurate 'universal' information. If offering opinions, make sure they are not confused with facts by stating that it is your opinion: '*In my opinion, when the issue of gender equality is talked about, some managers tend to freeze*'. Separating facts from conclusions is a challenge, but it is extremely important. It is a lot more difficult to argue with facts – as will be explained below when talking about non-violent communication. Facts are specific, objective and verifiable. Interpreting words and behaviour happens very fast: '*Jo doesn't trust me*' is a conclusion, not a fact. Facts are not controversial and provide a safe beginning. Facts are more persuasive than subjective conclusions.[3]

Communication styles and attitudes

Each person has a particular communication style that becomes an intrinsic part of them. There is no 'neutral' style. Culture is a big influencer of communication style. And whatever style you have or adopt, it will influence your audience. The more you are aware of your style, the more you can adapt when necessary. For instance, if you usually tend to try to argue your point and want to be right, you may hinder useful discussions. As authors Al Switzler, Joseph Grenny and Ron McMillan noted, 'Winning is a dialogue killer: we correct the facts, quibble over details and point out flaws in the other persons' arguments'.[4] As discussed in Chapter 4, experts often seek to win. The fastest way to kill a negotiation is to put two experts face-to-face, because an expert functions with a logic of truth, whereas a negotiator functions with a logic of interest. And in this specific case, the question remains:

is it better for you to get what you want (together with the relationship, as the relationship is what is needed to ensure the partnership will be respected) or to be right? Mentally step out of an argument, and watch yourself and the impact you are having. Stay humble enough to realize that you don't hold a monopoly on the truth and that you don't always have to win. The aim is not to be persuasive or to convince others that you are right. The aim is to find out what needs to happen for you to reach your goal. Being open, flexible, confident and cooperative will influence the way people communicate with you.

On being vague and uncertain

Avoid vague and uncertain words ('*I would like a bit more…*', '*I think less…*', '*Maybe…*', '*Something like…*') as they are too general for a successful negotiation. Instead of asking for 'more' salary or 'more' vacation, it is important to be specific. Do not leave anything to the other party's imagination or assumption when negotiating. For instance, instead of '*Could you work a flexible week?*' say, '*I would be most happy if you could work shift hours, with one week starting at 7am and finishing at 3pm and the next starting at 11am and finishing at 7pm.*'

Only when the request is precise can an answer be accurate. Whenever you are vague you are letting the other party interpret the non-specific request, which they will gladly do with *their* own interest in mind, and not yours (i.e. they hear what suits them). Being clear does not mean being pushy, it means… being clear.

- It is not because we do not want the same thing that we are in conflict.
- Not agreeing does not mean lacking respect.
- Listening does not mean losing.
- Understanding the other's point of view does not mean accepting it.

Everything that is said on both sides of the negotiation table, and even what is not said, conveys meaning and creates a reaction, including the words that are used, body language, facial expressions and tone of voice. So make sure that you convey what is in your best interest to convey. Being very aware of this will increase your influence, enhance your fine reactions and allow for better adaptations to even subtle changes of circumstances or attitudes. Micro-behaviours[5] play an important role in creating trust (see Chapter 9 for more information on micro-behaviours and their influence).

Communication skills – and most importantly listening skills – are fundamental to getting a good and lasting result in your negotiations. This is particularly challenging because when you finally, after a lot of energy, in-depth thought and analysis, have come to a good understanding of what you actually want to achieve, it is easy to fall into the trap of doing every-thing you can to try to convince your counterpart of the importance and righteousness of what you want. However, if you choose to negotiate, which *is* a bilateral approach, in which there *is* another party to take into account, then you must focus on and understand their needs, even if they are not clearly expressed and may therefore take some time to unravel.

Some models of behaviour and communication are particularly helpful during negotiations. Many excellent books and courses exist on the subject, and the aim here is not to give an in-depth explanation on them, but to share a few tips that could really help you during your encounters.

A useful communication model to help you during your encounters: non-violent communication

Marshall Rosenberg[6] observed that a lot of misunderstandings and conflicts arise from the fact that many people do not know how to adequately express their needs or emotions. He makes several points worth mentioning within the context of a negotiation.

'I' language versus 'you' language

The way people speak influences reactions. When upset, unfortunately people often use '*you*' language in a fairly accusatory finger-pointing way: '*You didn't wash up*', '*You put the wrong paper in the printer*', '*You never listen*', '*You always want to have your own way*'. 'You' language tends to create a closed or knee-jerk, even at times aggressive, reaction. This accusa-tion, combined with the generalization, is a quick way to create a defensive response, which tends to be counterproductive and often leads to escalation. Such an accusation may lead to an internal thought process response that resembles: '*Well as I am always lazy... why change – Jo will never believe I am capable of something different.*'

Two things are to be avoided at all costs:

- using *you* language – pointing an accusatory finger (*'You are so lazy'*)
- using generalizations (*'You never listen'*, *'You are always late at our team meetings'*)

When necessary, for example if you want to give feedback or share a concern, concentrate on how you feel, i.e. on *'I'* language, referring back to how one feels (*'I feel upset, unsettled, confused'*), as explained below; and on facts that are universal and observable, and definitely not what you conclude or imagine. Conclusions are based on interpretations, which can differ from person to person.

Rosenberg elaborated a four-step model for communicating one's feelings and giving feedback.

1 State facts (not conclusions or assumptions or generalizations).

2 State how *you* feel (the emotion when X is done, which is why this relates to 'I' language, i.e. *'I feel angry, disappointed, upset...'*).

3 State *your* need.

4 Offer a concrete request (which is not a demand).

EXAMPLE

Imagine the following discussion you are having with your teenager:

'You are always on your phone when we are having dinner! And I am fed with having your virtual friends at the table and never a moment of discussion with you.'

Instead, try:

'The last three evenings you were on your phone a lot during dinner time, and it upsets me. I need to feel that you appreciate the time and effort I took to prepare dinner. Could you please avoid using your phone at the table whilst we are eating?'

In a professional environment you might wish to avoid talking about feelings but to concentrate instead on impact, i.e. the impact a certain fact is having.

> EXAMPLE
>
> *'I have noticed that you have arrived 15 minutes late for the last three lab meetings (fact), which has meant that we need to spend time bringing you up to date on the discussion, which makes us run late (impact)...'*

In certain situations you could choose to avoid offering a concrete request, in order to leave room for creativity and development – in other words, let the other party think about what could be done to stop hurting one's feelings or to creating a situation that is hurtful.

Jackal and giraffe ears

Marshall Rosenberg talks about the many pitfalls people fall into when communicating that can hinder efficient respectful communication and hurt relationships, which should be avoided during negotiations.

Rosenberg notes people have a tendency to hear what is said through various filters, for which he uses the metaphors 'jackal' or 'giraffe' ears.

To put it very simply, the jackal metaphor indicates tendencies to dwell on criticism, judgement, bitterness and resentfulness, and the giraffe metaphor indicates being like a subtle translating device, rising above the emotion to understand the underlying need (realizing that behind every emotion there is an unstated and at times frustrated need that is being expressed in an unfortunate way).

When communicating, Rosenberg says that each person has four ears with which they hear any difficult message:

- *Jackal in ear:* Indicates the tendency to hear anything that is said to you as criticism, to take it personally and negatively, or to turn any message into self-deprecation: '*I am useless, I am so thoughtless, I never understand, I am...*' – i.e. '*There is something wrong with me*'.

- *Jackal out ear:* When using this ear you react to most messages by criticizing the sender: '*Jo is always complaining, Jo is never happy, the management is useless, the government is not doing their job...*' – i.e. '*There is something wrong with the other, the other is the problem.*'

- *Giraffe in ear:* With this ear you are aware of and hear your own (underlying) needs and, when appropriate, voice them: '*When she says she needs quiet time I feel insecure, so I need to make sure it has nothing to do with me asking too many questions or talking too much.*'

- *Giraffe out ear:* This ear enables you to sense the need behind the emotion that the other party is expressing, to understand that the emotion is hiding something deeper: '*When my colleague snaps at me, I sense that there is a deep feeling of unfairness rather than anger at me.*'

However simple these may sound, and you can read about them and study them in depth, they are challenging to put into practice; yet adopting the giraffe ears and avoiding *you* language will make your communication style more cooperative and efficient.

Verbal, non-verbal and para-verbal communication

As communication theorist Paul Watzlawick pointed out, everything is communication: 'one cannot not communicate'.[7] Different manners of communicating exist: signals and messages must be coherent, whether they are verbal, non-verbal or para-verbal. People notice a discrepancy or lack of coherence between what you say and how you say it, and will react accordingly, even if unconsciously.[8] Aim to be aware rather than to seek to control, and keep checking: are you giving the signals and messages you want to give? Focus on what you say and how you say it, on who you are, on what you show and on what you communicate without words.

CHARACTERISTICS OF VERBAL, NON-VERBAL AND PARA-VERBAL COMMUNICATION

Verbal communication is made up of the actual words you use.

Non-verbal communication is your own silent communication style, which is made up of:

- o your gestures
- o your expressions
- o your posture (more on posture can be found in Chapter 9)
- o the way you use space and move
- o your clothes and accessories
- o the eye contact you make
- o your smile

Para-verbal communication is how you say what you say:

o   your tone and speed of voice

o   your silences

All of the above make up your own specific communication style and should be coherent. When you 'sense' something is discordant in what the other party is saying to you – for instance, non-verbal signals are not synchronized with the spoken word – this might indicate that there is a hidden agenda, or something upsetting or disturbing them. And remember that whilst you are trying to learn from the other via their communication style, they are doing exactly the same to you.

It is a well-known fact that when communicating orally the non-verbal aspects play a much more important role than the purely verbal content. Professor Albert Mehrabian is famous for having researched the effect of non-verbal behaviour such as facial expressions, tone of voice and the literal meaning of the spoken word when communicating emotions and attitudes (for instance whether you like or dislike something or someone).[9] Mehrabian's early theoretical works and experiments demonstrate the role non-verbal communication plays in the expression of feelings towards others, particularly when there is a discrepancy between what is said and the accompanying non-verbal cues such as tone of voice or facial expression. He found that when words do not match the facial expression, people tend to believe the expression they see rather than the words they hear.

Specifically applicable when talking about feelings or attitudes, Mehrabian's theory states that:

- 7 per cent of the message is in the actual words that are spoken
- 38 per cent of the message is conveyed through para-verbal (paralinguistic) communication
- 55 per cent of the message is conveyed through facial expression

The way you say something will linger a lot longer than what you actually say. The value of his theory relates to communications where emotional content is significant, and the need to understand it properly is great, which are particularly important when negotiating. Non-verbal communication would thus represent more than 90 per cent of what is transmitted by you to your interlocutor. Who you are, how you feel, your micro-behaviours, your expression and what emphasis (tone) you put on your spoken words form an important part of your communication with others. A lot is communicated through your body and facial expression. The more coherent your non-verbal language and your micro-behaviours are with the spoken word, the more you build trust and security, which are two fundamental aspects to a useful discussion.

People pay more attention to those who convey that they mean what they say (because they show it – e.g. tone of voice, passion, facial expression, micro-gestures). And because communication is more than a matter of words, being also *how* the words sound, *how* they come alive, the fact that your goal is inspiring and meaningful to you will come across and will influence others. Furthermore, the fact that you really want to achieve your goal, that you believe in it, will impact your confidence level, your general attitude and your posture. This in turn will convey a strong message to your interlocutor.

It is easy to forget what tone of voice can do to the spoken word. Your mindset will be an influence: aim to seem (and be) confident, rested, at ease, 'engaged' in your aim and in the negotiation. Your behaviour is important and will be noticed. When in doubt as to what to do or how to behave, always ask yourself, '*Is it in my best interest to do such and such?*' This can be challenging and involves a fair amount of self awareness, for instance of one's true intentions.

Being extremely focused on the other, aware and observing very closely the way people communicate will give you a good advantage in negotiations, and will help you, for instance, sense whether something is negotiable or not, or whether a stated limit could in fact be flexible (e.g. through a hesitation, a discordant facial reaction, a worried glance at a colleague…). Remember, however, to assume nothing; instead, always test and question an assumption.

EXAMPLE

If you sense a hesitation or unease when talking about putting into place service level agreements, you might say: '*It seems to me that the service level agreements are a delicate subject and one that requires more time to discuss…, is there anything else you would have wanted to have included?*'

Posture is an important trait for a good negotiator – it affects how you come across to others. You cannot and should not fake experience and expertise, but you can fake a certain amount of confidence, which can help you[10] (see Chapter 9 for more information on this topic).

Non-verbal and para-verbal communication are culture-dependent, as has been noted previously (see Chapter 4 on contextual analysis). In these situations, make sure that when you are carrying out your contextual analysis you spend the time required finding out as much as possible about the way the other cultures tend to communicate. This will also be helpful to show that you are listening and respectful. It is so incredibly easy to get upset by a behaviour because it is interpreted as being disrespectful when in fact it could simply be a lack of knowledge or understanding. For instance, people from some cultures tend to be more blunt than others, others tend to keep very straight faces throughout... examples of such differences are abundant.

In the BBC's interesting article 'Why meeting another's gaze is so powerful' it was noted that eye contact shapes your perception of the other person who meets your gaze. For instance, in Western cultures people who make more eye contact are generally perceived to be more intelligent, more conscientious and sincere, and therefore are more inclined to be believed. Of course, too much eye contact can also make some people uncomfortable, and people who stare without letting go can come across as creepy.[11]

Chapter 7: summary points

- Throughout the encounters, remember that you need the other party. It is therefore in your best interest to learn as much as possible about them, to find out what they like, what they need, what they value, what is important to them, what they have misgivings about. The more you know about them, the more you will be able to work with them in an effective way. And the best way to find out is to ask.

- Make sure you are really clear in your mind on what you want to say and achieve. Use your roadmap, with your goal always in mind. The more prepared you are, the more confident you become, the clearer your message will be and the more creative you will be.

- Say what you would like to achieve from this negotiation, clearly and simply. Ensure you also communicate your cooperative style together with your willingness to be flexible and to explore options. You cannot expect the other to guess or mind read. Speak in a confident, open manner, and keep in mind that no commitment is made during the encounters, a fact that should lessen the pressure you might feel and – consciously or not – put on the other party.

- Avoid scenarios at all costs, i.e. mental conversations such as '*If they say this then I will say that, and if they mention this then I will …*' because these scenarios will influence the entire dynamics of the discussion and the way you interpret what the other party says.

- Keep in mind that if they don't know what you want they can't help you get it, and if you don't know what they want you can't help them get it. This sharing of information is crucial to be able to enter into the dynamics of exchange (rather than simply trying to convince them to give you what you want in a unilateral way).

- Rather than making assumptions, keep in mind that the best way to find out something about someone or about a situation is to ask questions. Ask questions until everything is as clear as possible.

- There is no need to justify or to apologize for your views and your wishes. At times you might wish to explain a position or a point, but justifying often involves the feeling of having been accused of something and thus needing to argue your point. When talking with those holding opposing opinions, the more convinced and forceful you are, the more resistant others become; the more tentatively you speak, the more open people become to your opinions. It is difficult to be attacked for what you didn't say. Think carefully before you share opinions as they can lead you into a debate that might not be helpful. Avoid humour as it can hurt and backfire.

- There are several quite simple yet powerful communication tools that, linked with verbal, non-verbal and para-verbal language, convey strong messages and give information. Make sure, however, that the verbal and the non-verbal messages you send are coherent with one another.

- Avoid small and belittling words (*more or less, almost, something like, ummm…*) and use your non-verbal language in a way that will help create trust.

- When faced with a possible blocking point, observe, stay attentive, concentrated and be patient. Remember that creativity and an open mind will create opportunities, whereas convictions create prisons.

- It is never a constructive idea to embarrass, humiliate, provoke or under-estimate anyone during the encounters. The most common reactions when faced with such behaviours are to shut down and disengage in the process or to become aggressive. And if such a situation happens, keep in mind that when faced with anger, aggression or silence (withdrawal), the best option is to try patience and curiosity and make sure you restore safety before continuing.[12] When there is anger, come to a mutual agreement to take time out. Never negotiate when angry. Always watch very carefully for signs that trust and safety are deteriorating.

- Building rapport with the others is important. This will ensure the process moves forward, as you listen more to those you like and with whom you can identify. Pay careful attention to those 'utterly unimportant words'[13] as they can mean a lot ('*Hello, how are you?*'). These often convey much more than you can imagine, such as acknowledgment and recognition, and are useful for building a relationship.

- Keep in mind at all times that the other party is an opportunity. Encourage others to express facts, feelings and stories, and carefully listen to what they have to say. This might take some time so be patient when possible.

- Remember, though, that even if you do everything by the book and still the other person doesn't want dialogue, then dialogue won't take place. It is worthwhile persisting, at least to begin with, not taking offence but being resilient, continuing to show respect. Keep believing that finding a way forward, a solution, is possible. Remind yourself of Nelson Mandela's resilience that guided so many of his actions, deeply aware that something always seems impossible until it's done. At some point the other will almost always join you in dialogue. And if they don't *at this time*, it means that they *currently* have no interest in pursuing the discussions, but that in the future the possibility to negotiate may arise again. In her book *Big Magic: Creative living beyond fear*, Elisabeth Gilbert refers to the fact that many people follow the tendency to let go and give up the moment things stop being easy or rewarding.[14] Resilience will stop you having regrets that you did not try everything and that you gave up too soon.

Notes

1   See Chapter 8 on online negotiations

2   S Cain (2013) *Quiet: The power of introverts in a world that can't stop talking*, Broadway Books, New York

3   K Patterson, A Switzler, J Grenny and R McMillan (2012) *Crucial Conversations: Tools for talking when stakes are high*, McGraw-Hill, New York

4   *ibid.*

5   C Arnold. What are micro-behaviours and how do they impact inclusive cultures? The EW Group. https://theewgroup.com/micro-behaviours-impact-inclusive-cultures/ (archived at https://perma.cc/62C2-Y59R)

6   M Rosenberg (2015) *Nonviolent Communication*, 3rd edn, Puddle Dancer Press, Encinitas, CA

7   P Watzlawick. Watzlawick's five axioms. www.wanterfall.com/Communication-Watzlawick%27s-Axioms.htm? (archived at https://perma.cc/5XHG-MQFB)

8   J-J Crèvecoeur (2000) *Relations et Jeux de Pouvoir*, Jouvence, Rumilly

9   A Mehrabian, www.bl.uk/people/albert-mehrabian (archived at https://perma.cc/E3AC-PZWH)

10   A Cuddy. Amy Cuddy TED talk: Fake it till you make it, YouTube, 2016. www.youtube.com/watch?v=RVmMeMcGc0Y (archived at https://perma.cc/3LJ2-8FG2)

11   C Jarrett. Why meeting another's gaze is so powerful, BBC, 2019. www.bbc.com/future/article/20190108-why-meeting-anothers-gaze-is-so-powerful (archived at https://perma.cc/BQC9-EB3L)

12   Inspired by K Patterson, A Switzler, J Grenny and R McMillan (2012) *Crucial Conversations: Tools for talking when stakes are high*, McGraw-Hill, New York

13   S Misteil (1997) *The Communicator's Pocketbook*, Management Pocketbooks, London

14   E Gilbert (2015) *Big Magic: Creative living beyond fear*, Bloomsbury, London

08

Online negotiations and online encounters

This chapter explores the usage and effects of online tools on the negotiation process. This topic came to prominence in 2020 when, due to the sanitary situation with the COVID-19 pandemic, the world became increasingly characterized by mediated communication, i.e. communication that is carried out through a medium that does not involve being in physical presence with the other.

What are the advantages and disadvantages of virtual encounters? Are outcomes influenced by whether the meeting happened in physical presence or not? Do emails and text messages help people to negotiate? What needs to be taken into account when running meetings via an online application? This chapter will suggest some answers.

E-negotiations and the corresponding tools (eNS – electronic negotiation systems) that encompass a decision-making system will not be covered. Such systems are mainly useful because, as complexity increases, human negotiators face problems understanding and evaluating all possible solutions and are regularly confronted with information overload in complex situations.[1]

Throughout this chapter, online negotiations will refer primarily to negotiation encounters that take place in part (a so-called hybrid format) or wholly via an electronic means, and that use electronically mediated communication (EMC) such as a computer with a video-conferencing application or emails. The focus thus will be on how to make the most of and to translate face-to-face negotiations into an online format simply and effectively.

Mediated communication also includes telephone, SMS and instant messaging.[2] It refers to an individual's ability to use communication technologies appropriately and effectively, so the tips presented in this chapter will be useful to those who are less digitally literate as well.[3]

The first part of this chapter touches on the context leading to the surge of online encounters. Next, considerations as to when to use electronically mediated communication – whether video-conferencing, emails or chats – will be developed. Then the chapter explores which EMC tool is best used for which step in the five-step negotiation process. Negotiating online through virtual encounters has specificities that need to be taken into account for maximum success and efficiency.

Whilst online communication has many advantages, for instance it is less expensive than travelling, and long-distance discussions are often easier to organize, there are also challenges to be aware of that must be taken into account. Some of these challenges will be explored, as will ideas on how to ensure the tools are used well. The characteristics and drawbacks of using emails when negotiating will be considered, and the final part of this chapter will focus on some of the advantages and challenges to bear in mind when engaging in online negotiation encounters.

Context of increasing reliance on online meetings

The outbreak of the COVID-19 pandemic in early 2020 considerably altered the way people do business, collaborate, negotiate and communicate, speeding up a process of digitalization that was already under way. People are increasingly relying on information technology and EMC to run their businesses and to replace face-to-face meetings. 2020 became an 'online revolution year'.

The use of electronic communication tools has never been so widespread and many have realized that it can be critical to the survival of many companies to embrace online negotiations. A widespread current belief is that, for many information-oriented workers, home working or virtual working is likely to become a long-term trend. Indeed, the advent of multiple video conferencing tools allowing hundreds of people to attend and interact in virtual meetings and conferences has changed the business outlook.[4]

With the increasing use of internet and of EMC technology, a lot of negotiations have, for many years, already been using electronic communication for planning meetings, setting up agendas, sending summaries and checking the status of a specific point. Author Maureen Guirdham, in her research on the topic, noted that before online tools – and in particular high-quality video conferencing applications – became widely used, negotiations in physical presence were widely preferred to telephone or email-based ones. She pointed out that the main reason for this was that face-to-face communication allows immediate feedback, provides multiple cues and uses natural language, thereby decreasing ambiguity far more quickly than any other means.[5] However, these advantages are increasingly possible with high-quality video conferencing applications, which combine voice and image so that people can talk whilst seeing each other. In video conferencing and in face-to-face situations, visual cues are constantly used to check for understanding and build rapport, which is not possible with memos, texting and emails.

Organizations, companies and governments are comprised of people who need to meet, discuss, negotiate and collaborate, whether or not this is possible in physical presence. Interconnectedness is as fundamental as ever in order for economic, political and social life to carry on. Negotiations continue to take place, partnerships to be built, collaborations to be set up, both online and offline. For example, the Brexit negotiations continued – albeit at a possibly slower rate – during the first period of lockdown in spring 2020, as did the negotiations surrounding the pricing and distribution of COVID-19 vaccinations between scientists, universities, pharmaceutical companies and governments.

E-meetings are rapidly becoming commonplace and usual for many people and communities. The need to re-invent the way people work, govern and function has become a question of survival. It is, however, important to remember that this new way of working requires a relatively high level of digital literacy and technical means that are not available to all to the same extent. Embracing this change – while being aware of its drawbacks – can be an enriching experience and a means to survive, because the current world situation has drastically reduced face-to-face encounters and travel. It seems reasonable to assume that 'business as usual' will never revert to a pre-2020 level and that the use of online tools will continue to expand, with meetings in future taking place virtually to a much greater extent, making EMC even more important.

What characterizes electronically mediated communication?

EMC varies, according to the tool used, in its capacity to transmit non-verbal cues, provide rapid feedback, convey personal traits and support the use of natural language. To help classify these differences, a theoretical framework called media richness theory (MRT) qualifies EMCs with respect to their 'richness' in conveying meaning that is not only semantic. Some EMCs provide a stronger capability for exchanging information effectively. For instance, email or chat will be less rich than video conferencing because the latter enables the communication of body language, facial expression and immediate feedback, and is therefore the closest to face-to-face communication.[6] For running encounters online and for negotiating, it is always better to choose those media that have a high richness and that enable multi-dimensional communication.

Social cognition, which is the overall process of observing and trying to make sense of other people, is important in a negotiation context. People gather information both from the content of the messages and from the way the message is given, i.e. through the non-verbal and para-verbal language. In her extensive research on the subject of mediated communication, Guirdham further points out that accuracy in social cognition is highly useful, at times vital, as it influences decision-making and communication. As messages can be – intentionally or not – ambiguous or contain multiple meanings,[7] the higher the MRT the less likely people are to make mistakes and false interpretations.

There are advantages and challenges inherent to this changing and growing use of technology to enhance or even replace communication between people. A clear idea of some of these advantages and challenges will help ensure EMCs are used in the most efficient way while also leaving space for emotional and social cues. Keep in mind also that the choice of communication medium will itself also be interpreted, as will any (sudden) change in communication medium. It could be useful to ensure that at some point early in the encounters you talk about 'meta communication', which refers to communicating about the way you communicate, clarifying what media you will use when and for what kind of information, thus setting some useful ground rules.

The different channels and their main decryption characteristics are – in order of richness (MRT):

- face-to-face: enables verbal, non-verbal, para-verbal language[8] decryption
- video conferencing: enables verbal, non-verbal, para-verbal language decryption (in a more limited way than face-to-face as peripheral vision – seeing what is happening outside the narrow lens of vision – is much more difficult)
- telephone: enables verbal and para-verbal language decryption
- text message and chat: enables verbal language decryption

As a general rule, when negotiating, if possible always choose the media that gives you the most cues to decrypt your counterpart's messages.

Which EMC tool can help in which step of negotiation process – and what is to be taken into account

Referring back to the negotiation process explained in this book, there are several steps in which EMC tools are readily used and have indeed proven their worth. The main electronic channels used when negotiating using this five-step process are emails and video-conferencing.

DURING THE CONTEXTUAL ANALYSIS STEP

During the contextual analysis step the following recommendations need to be taken into account.

It is important to make sure that all parties have access to a **good internet connection**. This will include connectivity and bandwidth, which is the data transfer rate of a network or internet connection.[9] The connection must be good – the last thing you want is to worry about the line going down. You should, however, allow for this possibility, particularly if you are negotiating with people in faraway countries with less solid connection capacity.

Computer ergonomics need to be taken into account. The parties involved in the meeting will need a computer screen large enough to be able to see all the participants in the encounter at the same time, together with a well-positioned camera and microphone. No one should be invisible. Lighting should allow for a good view of facial expressions. It is really important to see your counterparts. Remember that people constantly send behaviour cues which are stimuli to the senses and which are necessary to create an environment conducive to a solid respectful negotiation and to build a certain amount of trust.

Check before the encounters that the **technology** available to each party is as equivalent as possible so that there is little bias and unfairness due to unequal technology. This may include tablets, portable computers or personal computers and access to different applications. Technology must not be used unfairly to put one party at a disadvantage. One example is the use of a tool such as a touchscreen device, which allows the user to interact with a computer by touching the screen. This is a very useful add-on as it helps to jot down a graph, a note, a list in a natural way, as if you were using a flip chart or notepad. If one of the party does not have access to the possibility of writing and drawing to clarify an idea or a potential solution whilst the other does, understanding may be impaired. The same applies for sharing screens. The idea is to make good use of what is available and to have access to the basic tools that can support and enhance the discussion and understandings, rather than over-use fashionable tools or create an advantage of one party over the other.

You will need to make sure that all the parties who are involved in the negotiations have access to the **same software** with sufficient bandwidth, quality of image and sound. Software such as Microsoft Teams, Google Hangouts, Zoom, Go To Meeting, Cisco Webex and such like should be aligned. Depending on the payment of licences, some organizations, communities or people may not be able to access expensive software, and have to depend on open source software. This needs checking beforehand.

Digital literacy is going to play a role in how comfortable people are with the tools they will use. The less they struggle with the tools, the more they can concentrate on the discussion and the people. Video-conferencing platforms and online meeting solutions can be very user-friendly. Make sure you try both the internet connection and the functionalities before the encounters. Prior to the first online encounter, or at the start of it, it may be worthwhile and save a lot of problems later on to spend some time reviewing the basic options and functionalities if you think there may be some uncertainties with regards to mastery of the tools.

Confidentiality issues must be discussed and agreed upon by all the parties, for instance the decision about whether the encounter is going to be recorded or not, how and with whom the electronic documents are to be shared, and where (on what medium) they will be saved. Some of these points may be dictated by legal requirements. Make sure that safety and confidentiality issues are checked with regards to the rules and regulations of countries and the customs of organizations with which the negotiations and encounters will take place, as laws change from country to country. A quiet and private place is also important to ensure confidentiality.

Similar rules apply as they would in a physical encounter, with some additional ones such as putting on pause all notifications and closing all other applications so as not to get distracted. Experience shows that setting out and sending **online rules** prior to the encounters is useful (see below on the importance of sending an invitation). Depending on the parties involved, these can be discussed and formally agreed upon, or simply sent out with the meeting invitation.

All parties should be able and willing to receive **documents** during the encounter, go into **breakout rooms** if needed and turn on and off their microphone and video screens.

Roles will also need to be clarified just as in physical presence encounters: who is going to be the pilot, who the co-pilot, and whether experts will be on hand. In addition, some video-conferencing applications require additional – more technical – roles such as those of host and co-host. The decision of who is going to be host and co-host will also be decided, bearing in mind that these can change from one meeting to another: the parties can alternate hosting the encounters, promoting a sense of fairness. Depending on the number of participants it may be useful at times to name a facilitator, who could also be a co-pilot, to keep check on who wants to speak, for instance through raising a hand.

When setting up the meetings – at least before the first one – a clear **invitation** that is specifically tailored to the online format should be sent to all the participants. This invitation should set the framework on how the meeting will be run, including technological requirements, timing, confidentiality issues and any other logistical element that is necessary. This invitation should be sent by email.

DURING THE PREPARATION STEP

During the preparation step you might wish to ask yourself whether you will share your roadmap (see Chapter 5) on your screen, in which case you will need to prepare a copy *without your limits visible*. You might also decide to send some of your questions or information via email before the encounter, depending on the scope and complexity of the answers required. During the actual encounter they can also be sent via email for better understanding in multicultural contexts where mastery of the spoken language is not shared to the same level of proficiency by all participants.

DURING THE ENCOUNTER STEP

As seen in previous chapters, negotiations require discussions at some point, whether in physical presence or virtually. Thus when physical presence is not possible, an online alternative must be found. In order for negotiation encounters to be efficient and help build lasting agreements and partnerships, there are several points to bear in mind.

During the encounter step, which is when the online tools will have the most influence, it is important to remember that one of the skills that characterizes an excellent negotiator is their ability to build a relationship with the other parties, to observe – and act on – their emotions and non-verbal language and to pick up subtle sensory cues. Only face-to-face discussions allow for this dimension of communication to happen, whether face-to-face in physical presence or face-to-face via a computer with video such as Zoom, Microsoft Teams, Google Hangouts. Therefore, you should always try to organize at least one face-to-face encounter, preferably more.

Best practice 'in presence' meeting rules apply to online meetings too, such as respecting the agenda and timing, and naming someone to take the minutes. You will probably need to set rules for speaking (how to be noticed, who speaks when). The host/co-host roles need not necessarily be endorsed by the negotiation roles pilot/co-pilot. The pilot/co-pilot roles will be as important when online, with a particular emphasis on observing and reading the other parties' cues, body language and attitude. Be curious, ask questions, remain focused and make sure you concentrate on the other (and not on your own photo).

Building trust and social connection is fundamental, so make sure you spend sufficient time at the beginning of the meeting connecting with the participants – because the time usually spent having an informal welcome coffee or tea is not possible online. Even if building trust online might seem to be more difficult than in physical presence encounters, it is still possible. It can simply take a bit longer. Technology is only a tool – your personality matters just as much online as in physical presence. Opening the conference room 15 minutes before the start of the meeting can help, as long as there is someone available to welcome participants. You may choose to suggest that all notifications are put on pause so as to stay fully concentrated on the encounter, to listen carefully to what is being said and observe non-verbal cues.

Non-verbal language counts on screen as much as when you are in physical presence. The main differences are that on screen full body language is less apparent; usually only the face and shoulders are seen. Interestingly enough, using a camera can allow for more closeness and focus on the face, with its distinctive features and its expressions giving additional insights to your partner in negotiation. The way you sit, the clothes you wear, the background, the lighting, the expression of your face, your tone of voice – all will have an influence on the way you are perceived. It is important to remember that at all times you can be seen even if you are not talking. 'A distant, aloof air... may be acceptable, but seems even more cold and remote online. Be friendly!'[10] Keep sending belonging and social cues, such as smiling, keeping eye contact, nodding and find ways to show you are listening even more than when in physical presence. Ask many questions: they are a clear indicator of the depth of your listening and your wish to engage and understand.

Put as much attention into your dress code as you would if you were going to a live meeting and remember when you stand up to get a glass of water, people will see you entirely. Offline and online presentations should be consistent with one another.[11]

Before you enter the room, breathe deeply, smile, relax your shoulders and be as present in mind and body as you would be in a physical room. It is amazing how much can be felt and sensed via a screen.

Verbal and para-verbal communication play an important role when discussing negotiations via connected computers. People often talk too fast online. If you want to be understood, make sure you speak slowly and articulate well – even more slowly than in physical presence. You might wish to agree to a signal to be used when someone wants to talk, such as raising a hand. This will help avoid situations where several people speak up simultaneously as it can be difficult to see who starts talking when many people are online. In such situations, to ensure smoothness in the communication, someone will need to be assigned the role of moderator or facilitator. If you use an interpreter, make sure they have sufficient time to translate before speaking again. If the discussions require sign language, extra care will need to be taken with regards to the lighting.

Guirdham has found that emotionally positive negotiations are characterized by a higher number of exchanged words than emotionally negative interactions.[12] Therefore, engage in the discussion, using the same communication tools as described in Chapter 7. Differences between personalities can be exacerbated by 'online shyness' – where a person with an introvert tendency combined with online shyness may find it difficult to speak up, therefore being patient and showing your interest in an explicit way may be necessary.

Do not be afraid of silences. Silence and waiting for your turn to speak is even more important in online meetings because there may be a small time lag between what is said and other participants hearing. Don't jump to hasty conclusions when there is silence. As Guirdham points out, the longer pauses can be the result of technical delays and therefore should not necessarily have meaning attributed to them.[13]

Insist on clarifying and repeating what has been said and understood, on reformulating, and never hesitate to make several long breaks, as well as regular short coffee/stretch breaks. In online meetings, the time between breaks should be shorter than when you are in physical presence.

There are a few other considerations to bear in mind when meeting the other party online. Technology offers tremendous opportunities that can enhance the online experience. Do not just 'fall back on it' and simply convert 'in presence' to online. Use it to its full advantage. Not only will this make it more interesting, interactive and engaging, it will also ensure effective group dynamics are at play. Making use of breakout rooms for small group discussions or a bilateral conversation can help build trust and connection. Recording and filming the encounters, if all parties are in agreement, is useful in case you need to come back to a decision or to a specific part of a discussion, or if you need to share what has been said with absent people. Get this agreement in writing – to be checked during the contextual analysis step.

And at all times remember that not everyone is at ease with technology and that technology is a tool not a weapon.

DURING THE OFFER AND THE IMPLEMENTATION STEPS

During the two last steps of the negotiation process – the offer and the implementation, as well as during the encounter step, send memos and emails so that all participants share the same information. Whether the meeting is online or in person, it is always advisable to send a written summary so that everyone has the same factual record and can refer back to it if needed.

A few considerations on emails and what they should be used for

An email is an asynchronous communication medium, allowing for more reflection time between the message sent and the reply, thus decreasing the risk of knee-jerk reactions. Forming judgements, like forming impressions, takes longer by email. Since there is evidence that delaying judgements of others increases understanding of them, this asynchronicity may be beneficial.[14]

Emails are a tremendous help for certain tasks. For instance, they can be useful when there is a need to check a quick piece of information, to send a summary, to ask a question, to confirm a date, to send a reminder. In other words, emails are best used for a brief factual exchange. Emails can also be filed away for future reference in a straightforward way.

As discussed previously, when negotiating, words alone are seldom enough; written communication is not the best means for decrypting signs that will enhance understanding of the other party. If, however, you are involved in a negotiation that is taking place only or mainly in a written format such as for instance emails and memos, the following advice can be helpful:

- Do not assume your counterpart will read between the lines. Strive to state your emotions, feelings or concerns explicitly (*'I'm feeling frustrated about the lack of progress'*).

- Check in with counterparts regularly to see how they are feeling and check your assumptions: *'It seems to me that something in my last proposal upset you. Is that right?'*, *'How do you feel about this last discussion?'*

At times, written communication can be easier and more helpful when dealing with a party with whom you are in conflict, as it helps you to be more precise in what is written and to clarify misunderstandings; and it can be written away from the influence of emotions. Furthermore, written communication can be better suited to people with more introverted personalities.

It is interesting to note that people are fully aware of the importance of non-verbal communication to give subtle indications and convey meaning in a message, which is the main reason why emoticons and emojis were invented. People often use emojis and emoticons[15] to add some meaning into their emails, to replace – inadequately – non-verbal signals, and are aimed at sending a subtle (or not) message. Be extremely careful of this, as different emojis hold different significance in different cultures.[16] For instance, whilst the thumbs-up symbol may be a sign of approval in Western culture, traditionally in Greece and the Middle East it has been interpreted as vulgar and even offensive.[17]

Emotional and social cues are much more difficult to observe, to send and receive via email, thus hindering an important way of building trust and rapport. This will require taking more specific care as to the choice of words used. When writing an email, being extra careful with how to phrase an idea, how to make a suggestion, how to move forward will help reduce ambiguity and misunderstandings.

The written word cannot be erased, therefore make sure what you write and send is your true intention, and not an expression of anger or frustration that you might regret. Be careful of double meanings and always favour simple and straightforward language. No interpretation of what is written should be possible – hence the importance of being extra-careful in the way and in what you write. Remember: what you write can be legally binding, and some things, when taken out of context, can be damaging. Write first, leave to rest, re-read and *only then* send. Social cues and non-verbal communication are very hard to achieve via email although meanings and subtle messages are to be found in the actual wording used. Long emails or short factual ones, the way the email is signed, using a tone of regret rather than disappointment – all will convey a meaning to the written word and influence the relationship. The speed with which an email is answered also sends cues, as does the choice of words and details of the email.

At times people switch between emails and chats. The latter are to be avoided as they have a more informal touch and are less easy to save and refer back to. Depending on the sensitivity of the negotiation, chats should be considered unsafe.

Advantages of running negotiation meetings online

There are many advantages to running meetings and negotiations online. Many negotiations involve people that are based in different geographical locations. To be able to meet the other parties for a discussion takes time and energy, particularly when the people involved are based in different time zones. 'Travel fatigue' can hinder the quality of the encounters and influence the willingness of people to organize several meetings. Meeting in person can also be financially quite costly, often involving accommodation and travel expenses as well as administrative costs for the actual organization. With the possibility to use technology to connect with people around the world without physical face-to-face presence there can be considerable savings in money, time and energy.

People tend to be reluctant when things get complicated, as in, for instance, needing to coordinate people from different locations. Organizing several rounds of negotiations is simplified as there is no travel time to take into account. It is easier to block a half day and coordinate several agendas than a full day or even more. It is easier being flexible in finding dates – thus accommodating various needs (which can be a strong cue when negotiating) – when the meetings are shorter and online.

Recent world events such as the pandemic in 2020 have forced people to be very careful for health safety reasons when meeting in person. In most cases the sanitary situation even stopped people getting together physically. Online tools ensured that business could continue and that people could meet. If in-person presence meetings can only happen with participants wearing a safety mask, online encounters will be preferred as they enable a better view of faces, being able to lip-read and to observe non-verbal language better. Furthermore, some tones of voice sound quite muffled behind a mask, which, combined with possibly less expressive people, can make understanding more challenging. Finally, talking when wearing a mask can make understanding difficult if not impossible for people with hearing problems.

As discussed in the contextual analysis chapter (Chapter 4), multicultural settings can be tricky. Online encounters can help avoid possible mistakes or shortcomings linked with cultural customs, such as whether to shake hands or not, or the physical room set-up. For instance, there is no need to worry about who sits next to whom in online encounters. If this could be an issue when using breakout rooms, it is always possible with some video conferencing tools to assign people to the rooms manually.

It has also been noted that, as surprising as it may seem, some people actually find it easier to speak up online than face-to-face. The fact that they can be physically in the safety of their home can have an effect on their willingness and ease in talking.

Last but not least, it would also seem that there are strong ecological reasons for holding encounters online, particularly if flying is the chosen means of transport for international parties to meet.

Challenges and drawbacks of online negotiations

One of the most common drawbacks with running meetings online is that having access to full body language and peripheral vision in the room is more difficult. It has, however, been noted that 'interacting in a computer-mediated environment does not inhibit but merely decelerates the transmission of socio-emotional information'.[18] When online, facial expressions and para-verbal language are as fully communicated as in presence. Furthermore, at times facial expressions are even more noticeable as the camera can focus only on one person's face, enabling one to concentrate on the non-verbal in a more discreet way than in presence, where staring can be seen as rude and disrespectful.

Another drawback is the difficulty in engaging in informal small-talk as one cannot, for instance, move over to the coffee machine or step out for a breath of fresh air. Bonding and building trust therefore need to be carried out in alternative ways. For instance, although less discreet and spontaneous, it is often possible to send a more personal private message to someone, or to request a breakout room session. At times, depending on the complexity of the situation and your familiarity with the people with whom you are negotiating, you might wish, alongside the official encounters, to organize a bilateral informal discussion to get to know your counterparts better. Picking up the phone to call them between sessions is also a possibility, frequently overlooked and yet often appreciated.

Digital literacy is not shared by all to the same extent. Not everyone is at ease online, whether with the tools (technical savvy) or simply with the simple fact of being online. Extra care needs to be taken to include those who tend to 'fade away' into silence or get confused with the online tools and applications. If there is an imbalance in availability and mastery of online tools some people will be highly disadvantaged.

Although in some multicultural situations being online can help reduce the risk of mistakes (see above), at times it can make certain things more tricky. For instance, when negotiations take place in a multicultural context it can be more challenging to take on board cultural customs such as how people react towards time. Some cultures are more 'straight to the point' while others find it necessary to engage in more informal interactions and chats to create a trusting environment, without which negotiation is not possible. A Harvard article on overcoming cultural barriers in negotiation noted that:

> Westerners can become impatient as rituals and seemingly idle conversation with negotiators from Middle Eastern cultures drag out the process. From the other side of the table, however, such interactions are essential to building trust in negotiations. General cultural tendencies do not necessarily apply to specific individuals, of course, but it's wise to recognize that your counterparts may see time very differently than you do.[19]

Safety and confidentiality issues will need to be carefully checked, particularly if the various parties involved in the negotiations are spread around the world. Different countries have different laws, which can complicate certain negotiations that span borders. As discussed earlier, these aspects will need to be fully checked during the contextual analysis, talked about and agreed upon.

People behave and think differently and at different speeds whether online or in full presence. Beware of reacting too quickly; not everyone thinks and speaks at a similar pace. At times a reply may take a little longer than expected, or two people may (seem to) interrupt each other. As people tend to jump to conclusions and make assumptions very quickly, remember that connectivity might be the issue, or simply different personalities. In the article 'Online negotiation in a time of social distance', the Program on Negotiation of Harvard Law School warns that if your counterpart goes silent it is important not to automatically assume they're being difficult, or ignoring you just to gain an edge. Furthermore, they strongly suggest that you do not immediately take offence if a message seems abrupt or rude, but rather that you check in to enquire if there's anything they need. Remaining focused on the relationship at all times, and not only on the outcome, will help build trust rapport, and a more durable agreement.[20]

And finally, some people might get tired of sitting down and being in front of a computer screen and simply long for an encounter in physical presence.

Outcomes

Are there noticeable differences between the quality of the negotiated agreements if online or in presence? To date there is no evidence to suggest that negotiations conducted primarily – or entirely – online have better or worse outcomes than in physical presence negotiations. In her research, Rachel Croson concludes that:

> computer-mediated final agreements are somewhat more integrative than those negotiated face-to-face, suggesting there is no efficiency loss from negotiating long distance using information technology. Secondly, computer-mediated agreements tend to be significantly more equal than face-to-face agreements.[21]

What I have experienced is that mixing in presence and online encounters with electronic communication is very useful. Encounters in which the parties are participating virtually or in person should always be followed by email summaries and clarifying documents.

Chapter 8: summary points

- An online meeting platform is a tool and only a tool – relationships and trust need to be built whatever the means you choose to use.

- Smile before you start – you will be sending micro social cues to welcome the participants. Remember at all times that you are on camera being observed and that the focus is mainly on your face.

- In online meetings the same rules apply as they would in a physical encounter, with some additional rules such as pausing all notifications in order not to get distracted. Make sure these are communicated.

- Tools and technology are there to help and are great enablers, not to be hidden behind or used to 'score points' against people less knowledgeable or at ease. Digital literacy must be similar for all participants, when possible.[22]

- Depending on the scope of the negotiations and the complexity of the encounters, you might wish to suggest a short training session or send a link to a tutorial, being careful not to sound patronizing.

- Remain aware of and take into account differences between digital literacy levels and personalities (e.g. differences between how long people need to reflect and answer, fumbling with the technical options).

- Avoid treating online meetings as a second-class option. When well executed, the online experience, performance and quality can be the same as, if not better than, in presence.[23]

- Do not overdo the technology by using the latest fashionable add-ons. Make it human and stay simple.

- Online encounters should be shorter and allow for more short breaks to stretch and move around. Therefore during the contextual analysis plan for more time to reach an agreement.

- Remember time zones when setting up meetings with people around the world.

- It is possible and even advisable to at times simply pick up a telephone for a quick answer – a traditional means that is often overlooked.

- Make sure you test the internet connection and the functionalities before the encounters.

Notes

1   M Griessmair, P Hippmann and J Gettinger (2015) Emotions in e-negotiations, in *Emotion in Group Discussion and Negotiation*, ed B Martinovsky, Springer, New York. www.researchgate.net/profile/Leonardo_Christov-Moore2/ publication/300549098_Emotions_in_Interaction_Toward_a_Supraindividual_ Study_of_Empathy/links/5875508b08aebf17d3b3f6fd/ Emotions-in-Interaction-Toward-a-Supraindividual-Study-of-Empathy. pdf#page=110 (archived at https://perma.cc/QJ9Y-YWCZ)

2   M Guirdham (2015) *Work Communication: Mediated and face-to-face practices*, Palgrave MacMillan, London

3   M Guirdham (2015) *Work Communication: Mediated and face-to-face practices*, Palgrave MacMillan, London

4   M McLaughlin and D Brame. The best video conferencing software for 2021, PC, 2021. https://uk.pcmag.com/cloud-services/9067/the-best-video-conferencing-software (archived at https://perma.cc/32WF-75GL)

5   M Guirdham (2015) *Work Communication: Mediated and face-to-face practices*, Palgrave MacMillan, London

6   IG Global. What is media richness. https://www.igi-global.com/dictionary/ cultural-impacts-spread-mobile-commerce/18169 (archived at https://perma. cc/6CCL-NFVB)

7   M Guirdham (2015) *Work Communication: Mediated and face-to-face practices*, Palgrave MacMillan, London

8   See Chapter 7, Tools for use during encounters

9   Tech Terms, Bandwidth. https://techterms.com/definition/bandwidth (archived at https://perma.cc/2SM3-863C)

10 M Weller. The COVID-19 online pivot: Adapting university teaching to social distancing, LSE, 2020. https://blogs.lse.ac.uk/ impactofsocialsciences/2020/03/12/the-covid-19-online-pivot-adapting-university-teaching-to-social-distancing/ (archived at https://perma.cc/ WA9S-JP7V)

11 M Guirdham (2015) *Work Communication: Mediated and face-to-face practices*, Palgrave MacMillan, London

12 *ibid.*

13 *ibid.*

14 *ibid.*

15 The word emoticon is a portmanteau, made by combining the words emotion and icon. Remember, an emoticon is built from keyboard characters that when put together in a certain way represent a facial expression; an emoji is an actual image. Grammarist, Emoji vs emoticon. https://grammarist.com/ new-words/emoji-vs-emoticon/ (archived at https://perma.cc/YVZ4-GC6T)

16 A Fleeracker. Emojis in scholarly communication, LSE, 2019. https://blogs.lse.
ac.uk/impactofsocialsciences/2019/10/03/emojis-in-scholarly-communication/
(archived at https://perma.cc/FT6U-CD2N)

17 A Rawlings. Why emoji mean different things in different cultures, BBC, 2018.
www.bbc.com/future/article/20181211-why-emoji-mean-different-things-in-
different-cultures (archived at https://perma.cc/4UXB-QB57)

18 M Griessmair, P Hippmann, J Gettinger. Emotions in e-Negotiations. Available
at: https://www.researchgate.net/profile/Leonardo_Christov-Moore2/
publication/300549098_Emotions_in_Interaction_Toward_a_Supraindividual_
Study_of_Empathy/links/5875508b08aebf17d3b3f6fd/
Emotions-in-Interaction-Toward-a-Supraindividual-Study-of-Empathy.
pdf#page=110 (Consulted on 12 November 2020)

19 A Ojuri. How to overcome cultural barriers in communication: Cultural
approximations of time and the impact on negotiations, Harvard Law School,
2020. www.pon.harvard.edu/daily/international-negotiation-daily/telling-time-
in-different-cultures/ (archived at https://perma.cc/XC4L-GS78)

20 K Shonk. Online negotiation in a time of social distance, Harvard Law School,
2020. www.pon.harvard.edu/daily/negotiation-skills-daily/online-negotiation-
in-a-time-of-social-distance/ (archived at https://perma.cc/T73E-2V8R)

21 R T A Croson. Look at me when you say that: An electronic negotiation
simulation, *Simulation and Gaming*, 1999. https://journals.sagepub.com/doi/
abs/10.1177/104687819903000105 (archived at https://perma.cc/86Z8-B3BE)

22 The bandwidth of a medium is determined not only by the medium itself, as
posited by media richness theory, but also by the user – the more experienced
negotiators are with EMC, the more effective they are in encoding and
decoding messages and enriching the communication channel to convey
socio-emotional content. Thus, although the medium may impose certain
constraints on the interaction process, it is the way people make use of the
electronic bargaining table that primarily shapes the negotiation interaction.

23 M Weller, The COVID-19 online pivot: Adapting university teaching to social
distancing, LSE, 2020. https://blogs.lse.ac.uk/impactofsocialsciences/
2020/03/12/the-covid-19-online-pivot-adapting-university-teaching-to-social-
distancing/ (archived at https://perma.cc/XX3Z-V7TP)

09

Non-cognitive skills in negotiation encounters

The spoken word and non-verbal language, although very important, do not entirely capture what characterizes excellent negotiators.

In many ways, the two themes of this chapter are 'posture' and 'social intuition'. Posture is the output of emotions, concentration, stress and much more. The importance of posture and its influence on the dynamics of negotiating effective and lasting agreements is highlighted throughout the sections. Posture, behaviour, emotions, what you believe in and how you show it, how you communicate and engage with your counterparts, how comfortable, assertive and confident you feel and act will all have a strong influence on the outcome of your negotiations. They will also have an impact on the pattern of interactions and relationships you build and need in order to actually put the negotiated partnership and agreement in place.

Successful negotiations are highly influenced by the way the other party feels about you, whether they like and trust you or instead feel wary, whether they feel comfortable with the prospect of engaging with you or whether instead they are full of doubt and misgivings.

Purely cognitive elements are rarely sufficient to help understand why some negotiators are more successful than others. There is something else that affects the interactions and outcome of negotiations. This 'something else' has been called social intuition,[1] a skill that is believed to give the negotiator the ability to impact the entire negotiation.

To begin, social intuition and its effect on the negotiation encounters will be explained. Emotions have a big influence on how people interact, behave and communicate. The following section will explore the influence emotions have on interactions and interpersonal communication and shares some thoughts on how to manage them in such a way that they help rather than hinder the process. Finally, the effects of heightened concentration, stress resilience, positive self-esteem and high intuition on your negotiation encounters and outcomes will be explored. Careful preparation, communication skills and social intuition will together contribute to your success as a negotiator.

Social intuition and negotiation

Social intuition is an extremely useful skill for successful negotiations. In 2018, university professors Andrea Kupfer Schneider and Noam Ebner explored the concept of social intuition and its influence on negotiation encounters and therefore the negotiated outcome.[2] They defined social intuition as being based on the convergence of three skills:

1 the negotiator's capacity for self-awareness

2 the negotiator's capacity to focus attention on the other and find out information beyond what is conveyed explicitly

3 the negotiator's capacity to intentionally build bridges between themselves and their counterpart

Social intuition goes well beyond and encompasses more than verbal and non-verbal language. For instance, well-developed social intuition can lead a negotiator to sense when to slow their pace; when to communicate via email rather than picking up the phone; when to insist on a specific point or to withdraw momentarily. Social intuition varies from culture to culture, as it is strongly linked with non-verbal cues and behaviours that constantly send signals. Although very powerful when combined, these three skills are highly useful in themselves.

The first aspect of social intuition, the 'self', relates to self-awareness with regards to your own emotions, cognitive patterns, biases as well as your usual way of reacting. Two examples of why this skill is so useful are shared here:

- Stereotypes and biases often cloud judgements in an unconscious way. Being (more) aware of them will mean they become more conscious and therefore can be questioned and possibly readjusted.

- Referring back to the giraffe and jackal ears (page 107),[3] if you are aware of a tendency you have to react as a jackal, automatically finding faults with others and being on the attack quite easily, this simple awareness will enable you to question your automatic belief *'They are out to get me'*. If possible ask yourself *'What if I am wrong?'* and hence slow down your automatic reaction, possibly finding a more accurate way of responding.

Negotiators with high self-awareness are more likely than others to project clear and consistent messages and to recognize the effects that the others and the situation are having on themselves.

The second aspect, the **other**, is linked with the ability to read and under-stand your counterparts, being highly attuned to their emotional state and to how their state is reflected through their signals.[4] This capacity will give you valuable insight into the way your counterpart functions and will convey information beyond the spoken word. For instance, you might perceive micro-signals that your counterpart is approaching their limit. Andrea Kupfer Schneider and Noam Ebner further point out that at a very attuned level, these highly skilled negotiators might even 'be able to discern truth from lies, or recognize manipulative tactics, cloaked in politeness or affability, for what they truly are'.[5] As noted in Chapters 6 and 7, excellent listening skills are fundamental to being a successful negotiator. Often, when listening, answers are already being formed in your mind, reactions are already under way, whether consciously or not. Being able to listen in a highly concentrated manner, focused on what the other party is saying and not saying, as well as how they are expressing themselves, is going to help guide the interaction and encounters for better results – both in terms of content and of relationship.

The third aspect involves **bridging** – the actions that are taken to form connections in order to support the negotiation process. Schneider and Ebner explain bridging as follows:

> Bridging actions will likely include all sorts of micro-responses of which we might not even be aware as we are performing them. When this bridging works well, both negotiators look and feel as if they are moving together, even though substantive differences might still remain. The elements of situational awareness – the ability to read ourselves, read our counterpart, and read the situation – all come together as we take bridging actions.[6]

Emotions and stress management

The first two aspects of social intuition – self and other – involve awareness of one's own emotions and those of others. Emotions and their expressions guide and impact personal interactions and group dynamics. Poorly or inadequately managed, they can have an adverse influence on posture, behaviour, non-verbal language and therefore on the dynamics of the encounters that are necessary for negotiations to happen – whether online or in presence. Emotions also impact communication style as well as verbal and non-verbal language. People are constantly sending micro-behaviour signals that influence the way messages – spoken or not – are perceived. Emotions will also impact your own reactions. When angry, it is harder to listen and observe carefully, and easier to become more judgemental and impatient. When happy, it is easier to become so enthusiastic that details are not clarified and commitments are made too rapidly. When upset or disappointed, it is more challenging to be creative and believe in the possibility of a positive outcome. Fear can lead to aggressiveness or shut-down behaviour.

As Andrea Kupfer Schneider and Noam Ebner explain, when emotional tenor during a negotiation is monitored, the way you come across can be better controlled, such as whether the content of what you say matches up with your conduct, or if instead there are emotional 'gaps' between what you intend, what you say and what you do.[7] For instance, feeling fed up and discontented affects non-verbal language, which will show through subtle (or not) signals, such as becoming fidgety or yawning to indicate your bore-dom, keeping eye contact and staring to make the other feel uncomfortable, shifting your gaze, having your head level or tilted, or which can indicate – depending on your culture – uncertainty or irony and distrust. Micro-behaviours refer to these 'tiny, often unconscious gestures, facial expressions, postures, words and tone of voice which can influence how included (or not included) the people around us feel... and which can be verbal and non-verbal, very subtle, habitual, usually unconscious and influ-enced by our biases'.[8]

Have you ever noticed how a look or a change in behaviour can make you feel uneasy because of its intensity? A usual reaction when feeling under attack (whether the aggression is perceived or real) is to fight back. And as soon as you start fighting back, the other party is seen as an opponent, and you want to win. Micro-expressions of this change of attitude – *before even the spoken word* – will come across and be sensed, seen and felt by the people with whom you are negotiating and who – remember – you most need to have on board, and partner with. This change in energy will impact the dynamics of the discussions and therefore the outcomes of the encoun-ters. If you are overcome by emotions – yours or those of the people with whom you are negotiating – you might become more aggressive or upset than you would wish to be, you might take comments more personally, be more sensitive or judgemental, focus more on winning (the argument), and be less creative and open.

Being aware of one's emotions before they trigger an automatic reaction – which unfortunately is rarely the most appropriate one – is a skill worth developing for any negotiator. Because before emotions can be regulated, you first need to be aware of them.

One way to better manage one's emotions that is increasingly recognized for its effectiveness is regularly practising meditation and its derivative, mindfulness.[9] 'During mindfulness meditation, the meditator's goal is to maintain attention to current internal and external experiences with a nonjudgemental stance, manifesting acceptance, curiosity, and openness.'[10] Mindfulness – whether through meditation or not – involves being aware of what is happening at the physical and psychological levels, of physical sensa-tions and biological responses, however subtle they may be. It is moment-to-moment awareness, simply noticing and observing.

Why is this relevant and how can this improve your negotiation skills?

When you become aware of what is happening at the physical level, you notice the sensations as they arise. When you notice what is happening, you pause for a fraction of a second. This fraction of a second helps you avoid – or slow down – an automatic reaction, based on the trigger, thus creating a space in which the possibility for adapting your response lies. As psychiatrist and holocaust survivor Viktor E Frankl remarked, 'between the stimulus and the response there is a space and in that space lies our power and our freedom'.[11] When negotiating, you might react (very) strongly to something you perceive as unjust and automatically snap or close down. Passion, anger, desire, fear all colour your perceptions – you cannot see clearly. Often you do not even realize the impact these emotions have on your life. It is through creating this minute space that the negotiator can seek to adapt their response and attitude in order to remain solution-focused.

For example, during an encounter someone may say in an accusatory way, '*You are always bringing your expertise and past experiences to the table and we are simply not interested. You don't listen to us – you are always so closed to new ideas.*' You might sense your jaws clenching, or your hands becoming sweaty or tight-fisted. You might feel your stomach churn. Your gut reaction might be offended or hurt and therefore you have the urge to 'fight' (attack) back or 'flee' (get up and leave the table). By silently noticing what is happening, '*I am really upset by what has just been said. I have a knot in my stomach, my jaws are clenched*', you are exiting the automatic response syndrome, soliciting the more analytical part of your brain (the cortex). This will enable you to think of the most adapted response, which could be, '*I am sorry you feel that way. I do, however, strongly believe that we can learn from the past experiences of all those here present. Maybe we could think of a way to create some space for these that is acceptable for all, like for instance starting the meeting with some time for each to speak?*'

Although quite challenging, a regular – even short – practice of mindful meditation can and does help. When faced with strong emotions, 'body sensations serve to continually guide participants back to the present moment, for example, by redirecting one's attention to breathing sensations when the mind has become restless or entangled in the thought stream'.[12]

Having a better control over one's emotions is important for several reasons.

First of all, emotions tend to be contagious, affecting the mood of the encounters and the other parties.

Second, they influence what you say and how you behave. Coming back to the breath, inhaling and exhaling deeply when under attack (whether a real or even a perceived threat) helps you to keep calm under pressure and not overreact. Imagine you are getting seriously annoyed by someone constantly interrupting. If you manage your emotions, i.e. the anger, it will be less visible and you might just be more able to respond in a calm way (as a 'giraffe'[13]), stating for instance what your needs are with regard to being listened to in an uninterrupted way or asking for ground rules to be clarified for all those attending the meeting.[14] Whilst you are carefully observing the various parties around the negotiation table, *they* are also observing *you* and making their own interpretations of what they see and sense. It is therefore in your best interest to be aware and as careful as possible as to what you show – anchored, in control, at times smiling, always concentrating.

Turning towards emotions rather than away from them, acknowledging them first and then seeking to understand '*Why am I feeling what I am feeling?*', '*Is there something wrong that should be addressed?*', '*Am I missing something?*', '*Could there be a hidden agenda?*' can be extremely helpful, at times indicating that something is not as it should be in terms of the dynamics of the interactions during the encounters. This in turn will feed your intuition and give you valuable cues (see page 136).

In negotiation language, it is therefore *in your best interest* to find a technique to manage your emotions, meditation being just one of them.

An increasing number of scientists are researching the effect of meditation on general well-being.[15] These studies, many of which are based on MRI scans and questionnaires, all tend to point to the following results:

- heightened attention regulation and concentration
- increased body awareness
- better emotion regulation
- stronger stress resilience
- change in perspective of self with higher acceptance and more positive self-esteem
- better capacity for decision-making and creativity
- lower anxiety and depression
- decrease of negative mood states
- higher intuition

These benefits span much more than well-being, with noted effects on social intuition and negotiation. They are particularly relevant when negotiating and interacting with your counterparts. All are interlinked, each one influencing the other in a web of interconnectedness.

Heightened concentration and negotiation

Regular mindfulness practice enhances concentration, with a potential strong influence on three specific areas of the negotiation process. First, during the preparation steps (contextual analysis and goal analysis) being highly focused and concentrated will enhance the quality and creativity of your roadmap and contextual analysis. On page 143 we share some more insight on creativity.

Second, during the encounters you become much more concentrated on your own reactions, sensing your emotions and body sensations (for instance, this can be a clenched jaw or a sudden realization that you are holding your breath). Being more aware will in turn help you be more in control of what you show and your facial expressions, the micro-behaviour signals you send out. Third, you become much more concentrated on and aware of the others, of their non-verbal language, of what they say or do not say, of how they behave and communicate. It becomes easier to pick up cues, notice and check your intuitions and focus on more than simply the words that are used. Heightened focus and concentration will also lead you to be (slightly more) aware of micro-behaviours. As management consultant and author Peter Drucker noted, 'the most important thing in communication is hearing what isn't said'.[16] This heightened attention means you will be more aware of the dynamics of what is happening at the negotiation table.

Stress and negotiation

Many negotiations can be stressful because you are focused on wanting something important, maybe even at times necessary or vital. Think of the Brexit negotiations or, closer to home, the last time you were negotiating a job contract or a deal with a supplier – important moments that can be quite stressful. Coming across as tense, nervous, possibly fidgety or sweaty-handed are best avoided. Regular practice of meditation helps boost stress resilience. Researchers have noted that, at the neurobiological level, meditation has consistently been shown to reduce hormones that are known to trigger biologically based anxiety responses.[17]

Negotiating, particularly when the stakes are high, can breed anxiety, stress and impatience. These in turn can lead you – even unconsciously – to put pressure on others, to interrupt, to start bringing up arguments to try and convince them to change, to be more 'heavy-handed', thus entering in an argument/counter-argument dialogue. When this occurs, listening is impaired; careful listening to differing points of view and to your counterpart's concerns will at worst disappear, at best becomes less straightforward.

Successful negotiators can benefit from heightened stress resilience, which breeds a calm inner space. Furthermore, being more resilient to stress helps people keep a more positive outlook on life. This attitude affects optimism and a solution-focused attitude, generating – during the negotiation – trust that this agreement or contract will come through, that you will be able to negotiate this partnership, that you will find an outcome that will suit each party's (self) interest, that *it is possible*. Psychologist Daniel Goleman, who has studied emotions extensively, noted that emotions are contagious and high-energy, positive people tend to influence low-energy people.[18]

Being less prone to (high) stress and remaining positive are also going to have beneficial effects on resilience, the capacity to bounce back and keep trying, to not take a negative reply personally, to realize that a '*No*' today can become a '*Yes*' tomorrow. This solution-focused mindset will, when confronted with a negative reply, lead you to ask '*What would it take for you to say yes?*' instead of baulking or giving up immediately. Surprisingly, this is often a difficult and challenging question for your counterpart to answer, and can open up new opportunities to explore *the (new potential) conditions under which they would agree.*

Remember to be patient. Pushing your point across today may backfire – whereas waiting for a more appropriate moment will create new pathways. Resilience, patience and optimism make a strong team.[19]

Self-esteem and negotiation capacities

Posture is influenced by self-esteem and – when perceived as positive – will impact the outcomes of your negotiations. The way you feel about yourself will be translated into – at times micro and often unconscious – behaviours that come across through non-verbal language, facial expressions (readiness to smile, eye contact, etc) and the way you speak, the words you choose to use, your tone of voice, how often you ask questions and show curiosity. As mentioned previously, non-verbal communication (i.e. attitude, gestures, behaviour) have a strong impact and often convey messages better than words.

Have you ever noticed that when you go into a meeting feeling low, with little self-confidence and poor self-esteem, you often tend to achieve poor results? On the other hand, if you go in 'head held high', feeling good, anchored, balanced, things seem to go your way? You influence your results. Where you put your attention, you put your energy and creativity. Move from *'I am a failure, this will never work'* to *'I think it may be hard but it's possible and I'll do my best. It could work, why not?'*

Yet again, research findings have shown that regular meditation helps breed a more positive outlook on life and contributes to more positive self-esteem. Simple deep breathing can also help. Breathing and exhaling deeply triggers a biological response that lowers the heart rate and blood pressure. This in turn will make you more relaxed and calm during negotiations.[20]

If you are feeling positive and self-confident, you are embodying the fact that you believe an agreement can be reached, that the negotiation will succeed and that you can all partner in the process, that you really *trust* it is possible. You come across as highly trusting that an outcome, a solution, is possible. Confidence and trust are as contagious as optimism. Being positive during the encounters will enable more solution-focused dialogues, concentrating on finding solutions and building paths, on being creative rather than on problems and difficulties. Positive emotions are connected to positive social connections, which are fundamental to building lasting partnerships in a non-confrontational manner.

Intuition and negotiation

Social intuition, as discussed earlier, has a strong component of awareness of the other. This is enhanced by intuition. Scientific findings have shown that in people who meditate regularly there is a physical change in the structure of their brain, notably with regard to those zones that are linked with concentration, intuition and emotion regulation.[21] Intuition helps sense the mindset of the other party and notice micro signals that otherwise often go unseen. Intuition will indicate when the atmosphere is becoming uneasy or lighter, when the rhythm needs to be changed or when a break needs to be suggested, when it is better to 'let it lie' or insist slightly. In a Forbes article, Dina Kaplan shared her experience:

> because you reduce the thoughts in your mind when you meditate, you gain
> intuition and begin noticing subtle signals from people, such as when they
> look away, start playing with their hair or speak with a more emotional tone.
> Now my gut picks up on these cues and I sense, for example, when someone is
> sharing a key point.[22]

In their case study 'Nonverbal communication in negotiation',[23] Michael A Wheeler and Dana Nelson write about how much communication is not conscious, and therefore intuition is fundamental to pick up necessary cues. They conclude:

- We communicate far more information to other people than is conveyed by our words alone.
- Our non-verbal signals sometimes contradict the words we use.
- Much of this communication is less than fully conscious.
- Reading non-verbal communication is an art, not a science.
- Non-verbal communication must be understood in the context of the broader set of interactions among all parties.

Someone who meditates regularly picks up on things that are difficult to explain tangibly.

How creativity benefits from a calm mind

Chapter 3 presented the four prerequisites to be able to engage in a negotiation process, with one of them being creativity. Creativity is fundamental. First linked with thinking about your conditions and building your roadmap, creativity is also highly relevant during the encounters, how you see things and particularly the hurdles that are bound to occur. Seeing difficulties as challenges helps you to become less overwhelmed by them. Mental agitation contributes to more confusion. A calm mind contributes to more insight, which is invaluable when you need to make a balanced decision. Observing without judging, being simply aware, capturing even subtle signals all tell you a story, which, if listened to, will enhance the quality of your decisions and the creativity with which you try to find alternative paths to get to where you wish to go.

Focusing on possibilities and creative thinking, such as concentrating on what could be done to make this (solution, idea, etc) happen and avoiding problem-focused language will lead you to concentrate on more positive (solution-focused) language such as the hypothetical '*what if*' questions, the '*imagine we have signed this deal*' approach.

Being in a calm mindset and in an inner quiet space will also help you to keep a (slightly more) detached attitude, more observant and neutral, and help you to decide how you wish to behave, even if you do not appreciate what is happening. Staying as aware as possible of your state of mind, observing the dynamics of the encounters, consciously deciding not to 'plod on' but to take a break, go for a walk and come back refreshed, maybe even with a different outlook and appreciation of the situation, can often bring the best results.[24] Psychologist Alice M Isen remarked that positive emotions facilitate a broad range of important social behaviours and thought processes, leading to greater creativity, improved negotiation processes and outcomes and more thoughtful open-minded flexible thinking and problem solving.[25]

Chapter 9: summary points

- Being more anchored, more in control of your emotions and more open-minded will help you approach the other parties from a stronger, safer inner place and keep you aware throughout that your counterparts are *at the moment* your best opportunity and partners in negotiation. This will in turn breed a more trusting and solution-focused environment.

- Social intuition is a highly impactful skill to develop. Social intuition is based on self-awareness, awareness of the other and the capacity to build bridges between both, connecting with your counterparts.

- Social intuition differs from non-verbal communication. This latter focuses on encoding and decoding meaning based on certain non-verbal cues, whereas social intuition involves understanding a situation in a more complete way and *affecting it comprehensively.*[26]

- One way to develop social intuition skills is through regular practice of mindfulness, for instance through meditation.

- Being anchored in a focused, quiet inner space will influence your self-confidence and your non-verbal language. This in turn will be translated in micro-behaviour signals which constantly send messages to the people you are communicating and negotiating with, impacting their reactions and building trust.

- Being highly focused and aware of the others and of what is going on in a visible and less visible way will give you a tremendous advantage in picking up and acting on – if deemed the right thing to do – cues.

- Being aware of your own emotions and subtle reactions will indicate when and where you may wish to be more careful about what you show, be more in control of verbal and non-verbal language and possibly indicate that it is time to suggest a break, change the rhythm, insist or temporarily withdraw.

- Being intuitive and at times acting on your intuitions is important when negotiating. Remember at all times that intuitions can be checked, as '*I have a feeling that this proposal is/is not…*', '*It seems that there is some uncertainty about…*'.

- Listening in a non-judgemental way, being 'in the moment', focused on what the other is saying at all times will give you insight into what is truly going on.

- Connecting with the other, understanding not only cognitive factors but also emotional content will enable you to understand much better the other's perspective and the overall situation.

- Listening from a quiet inner place, anchored in yourself and your goal (roadmap), whilst remaining focused on what is happening, will help you be more creative. Getting overwhelmed or carried away by emotions (e.g. feeling threatened and getting scared or angry) clouds the mind and hinders creative thinking.

Notes

1   A K Schneider and N Ebner (2017) Social intuition, in *The Negotiator's Desk Reference*, ed C Honeyman and A K Schneider, Marquette University Law School, Legal Studies Research Paper Series, Research Paper No. 18-05

2   *ibid.*

3   M Rosenberg (2015) *Nonviolent Communication*, 3rd edn, Puddle Dancer Press, Encinitas, CA

4   A K Schneider and N Ebner, *ibid.*

5   *ibid.*

6   *ibid.*

7   *ibid.*

8   C Arnold. What are micro-behaviours and how do they impact inclusive cultures? The EW Group, https://theewgroup.com/micro-behaviours-impact-inclusive-cultures/ (archived at https://perma.cc/5MUE-YMML)

9   M Ricard and W Singer (2017) *Beyond the Self: Conversations between Buddhism and neuroscience*, The MIT Press, Cambridge, MA

10 B K Hölzel, S W Lazar, T Gard, Z Schuman-Olivier, D R Vago and U O Hoelzel. How does mindfulness meditation work? Proposing mechanisms of action from a conceptual and neural perspective, *Perspectives on Psychological Science*, 2011, 6, 6, 537–59

11 V E Frankl (1946) *Man's Search for Meaning*, Beacon Press, London

12 B Bornemann and T Singer. Taking time to feel our body: Steady increases in heartbeat perception accuracy and decreases in alexithymia over 9 months of contemplative mental training, *Psychophysiology*, 2017, 54 (3), 469–82

13 M Rosenberg (2015) *Nonviolent Communication*, 3rd edn, Puddle Dancer Press, Encinitas, CA

14 See Chapter 6 on the encounter, and Chapter 7 on non-violent communication techniques

15 B K Hölzel, S W Lazar, T Gard, Z Schuman-Olivier, D R Vago and U O Hoelzel. How does mindfulness meditation work? Proposing mechanisms of action from a conceptual and neural perspective, *Perspectives on Psychological Science*, 2011, 6, 6, 537–59; M Ricard and W Singer (2017) *Beyond the Self: Conversations between Buddhism and neuroscience*, The MIT Press, Cambridge, MA

16 P F Drucker. The most important thing in communication is hearing what isn't said, 2010. https://rantsandrevelations.wordpress.com/2010/09/26/the-most-important-thing-in-communication-is-hearing-what-isnt-said-peter-f-drucker/ (archived at https://perma.cc/38ZC-FPPD)

17 K W Chen, C C Berger, E Manheimer, D Forde, J Magidson, L Dachman and C W Lejuez. Meditative therapies for reducing anxiety: A systematic review and meta-analysis of randomized controlled trials, *Depression and Anxiety*, 2012 29(7), 545–62

18 D Goleman. Happy or sad, a mood can prove contagious, *New York Times*, 1991. www.nytimes.com/1991/10/15/science/happy-or-sad-a-mood-can-prove-contagious.html (archived at https://perma.cc/FR99-AZLY)

19 When outside conditions have changed so drastically, it is important to think on a strategic level about whether this is the right moment to renegotiate a partnership or whether there are other priorities to which you can adapt. Being able to adapt and being flexible doesn't mean giving up what you ultimately want; it means that at times it is in your best interest to postpone the request. R Bisson. Negotiation stations, Research Professional News, 2020. www.researchprofessionalnews.com/rr-funding-insight-2020-9-negotiation-stations/ (archived at https://perma.cc/77YK-YUZK)

20 C Bergland. The neurobiology of grace under pressure, *Psychology Today*, 2013. www.psychologytoday.com/intl/blog/the-athletes-way/201302/the-neurobiology-grace-under-pressure (archived at https://perma.cc/8GT9-SGPP)

21 Tibetan monks have heightened intuition. In 2008, New York University neuro-scientific researchers MRI imaged the brains of over 20 Buddhist monks during meditation. Some of the findings of these and other researchers include:

- Meditation can beneficially change the inner workings and circuitry of the brain, better known as 'neuroplasticity'.

- The happier parts of the brain (prefrontal cortex) were far more active.
- Their brains tend to 're-organize', which means they feel a sense of 'oneness' with the world around them.
- The brainwave patterns of the Buddhist monks were far more powerful, implying a higher level of external and internal thought.
- Their brains had enhanced focus, memory, learning, consciousness, and 'neural coordination'.
- The monks had no anxiety, depression, addiction or anything of the sort.

Eco Institute. The meditating monk's incredibly powerful brain. https://eocinstitute. org/meditation/buddhist-monk-meditation-2/ (archived at https://perma.cc/4BR6-6HX5

22 D Kaplan. Meditation: A secret superpower for negotiation, Forbes, 2016. www.forbes.com/sites/dinakaplan/2016/07/13/meditation-a-secret-superpower-for-negotiation/#251b40b4be6e (archived at https://perma.cc/5XED-JDY6)

23 M A Wheeler and D Nelson. Nonverbal communication in negotiation, Harvard Business Publishing, 2003. revised 2009, https://hbsp.harvard.edu/ product/903081-PDF-ENG (archived at https://perma.cc/F6T3-NELY)

24 D Vessantara (2017) *Tales of Freedom*, Windhorse Publications, Cambridge, UK, 166

25 F P Bannink (2010) *Handbook of Solution-Focused Conflict Management*, Hogrefe Publishing, Cambridge, MA, 91

26 A K Schneider and N Ebner (2017) Social intuition, in *The Negotiator's Desk Reference*, ed C Honeyman and A K Schneider, Marquette University Law School, Legal Studies Research Paper Series, Research Paper No. 18-05)

PART FOUR

Offer and implementation

The following two chapters will cover the final two steps of the negotiation process: step 4, the offer and step 5, the implementation. Once all the required prerequisites and conditions have been met, once you have all the information you need, once you have followed your roadmap and you know how your counterparts respond to *your* conditions, once you know what *their* needs and conditions are, then and only then will it be possible to step back and start thinking about making your first offer.

Chapter 10 examines step-by-step what needs to be done to first build and then present your first offer, and finally to reach the signed and approved agreement. Chapter 11 covers the implementation requirements for the agreement to be put into practice.

10

Step 4: the offer

Once you have said what you wanted, once you have explored the conditions under which your counterpart will agree in part or wholly to your conditions, once you have discovered what they want and discussed the conditions under which you would engage and agree to accept wholly or in part their conditions, then and only then can you start thinking about making an offer. The aim of step 4, the offer, is to build bridges between what you want and what the other party wants. This will involve drafting your first offer, presenting it, discussing it, and working on it to finally reach an agreement. It is the result of everything that has happened during the various encounters, anchoring what has been discussed in a commitment.

Once again, the negotiation process is iterative, so you might have several discussions using a first offer as a starting point, and then maybe working on several others. The ultimate aim is thus to come to a negotiated offer that is agreed by all parties, and in which all find some level of interest.

You will need to show patience and yet again resilience, at all times keeping faith that an outcome is possible. To quote Barack Obama, if you're walking down the right path and you're willing to keep on walking eventually you'll make progress.[1] Therefore, think carefully before you think of giving up.

First you will explore the prerequisites for being able to start building an offer, i.e. when you know you are ready to continue and move out of the encounter step. Building an offer is straightforward even though it requires some careful analysis. The next part of this chapter will take you through the necessary actions that will help you do this, and finally you will learn how the offers are to be presented and worked on.

Prerequisites and conditions for making an offer

There are certain elements that need to be in place before you can think about working on your proposal. The more efficient your encounters were, the easier this will be, as often the offer is little more than a formalization of what was discussed during the encounters. The two prerequisites to entering into this step are:

1 You need your roadmap **with the other party's reactions** to what you said, to your ambitions and to your conditions. For every stated ambition, did they say *yes*, *no*, *maybe*, did they hesitate, did you get the feeling they were flexible? This information is fundamental and no guess work is allowed.

2 You need to know what they want, what their goal is, what their conditions are, to have a good idea if the values they mentioned were flexible and negotiable or not. In other words you need to have the contents of their roadmap, which should be on your notes sheet.

At some point, you might feel the moment is right and that you have what you need to be able to work on a proposal that you believe will include all relevant conditions. The following three actions need to be taken when you want to engage in this step:

1 To begin this process, when you are still in the meeting, make a summary, explain that you are in a position to prepare an offer, and take a break during which you work on it. If you reach this point of readiness during

the encounter, **never prepare an offer in front of the other party** and instead wait until you have finished the dialogue and take a break. This is because you want to avoid making concessions or commitments you may later regret. Nor do you want to be seen to be reacting too quickly.

2 Next, **the environment needed to start thinking about your proposal** should be a quiet private location, where you can be alone or with your team if you have one, in a space conducive to thought. Remember never to elaborate an offer in front of the other party. Building an offer can be a lengthy and reflective process, even though it normally should be quite straightforward: everything should have been discussed during the various encounters. You step out, anchor yourself back into yourself and your roadmap, and analyse.

3 Finally, to build an offer and work through the following steps, you **collaborate with your team,** using your experts and your co-pilot when available.

If the various discussions have gone well and been thorough, building and working on a proposal is straightforward, as it is a formalization of what has been talked about and should contain no (or only symbolic or of little (financial) value) new elements. There should be no surprises, no 'bomb-shells' in your offer. In other words, there should not be important new conditions that have never been discussed and that will come as a total surprise to the others.

What to do once the prerequisites for making an offer have been met

During an encounter, there will come a time when you feel that you have all the information you need, that you have discussed your conditions, and the other party's conditions, and you have a good idea of what the potential agreement would look like. To be sure that you have not missed anything, after the final summary you might ask whether there is anything more you should know, or whether there is a last question the other party wishes to ask.

Then you retire – you move away with your team. You should always be careful not to leave anything lying around in the room that was used for the meetings and which could be misused.

When you are in your quiet place, the following actions need to be carried out.

10.2 **STEPS TO BUILD A FIRST OFFER**

1 CHECK

– *that my roadmap has been properly used*

– *that I have constructed their roadmap*
  (and know as much as possible what they want)

2 WEIGH

3 POSITION *THE OTHER'S REACTION*

4 *DECIDE ON* **STRATEGY:**
   IF I ACCEPT – AGAINST WHAT?

5 *DECIDE HOW I WANT TO* **REACT** *TO*
   THE OTHER'S NEEDS AND WISHES

6 BUILD OFFER: *IF YOU... THEN I...*

7 DECISION: *PURSUE OR NOT?*

Steps to build an offer

1. You check

You first check that you really have used your roadmap in a satisfying and complete way: did you actually tell them what your goal was (not '*Do I assume they understood it?*', rather '*Did I actually voice it?*')? Did you mention your vital and most important conditions *with their ambitions*? Did you give them the information you prepared and wanted to share? Did you ask the questions you needed to ask? In other words, did you effectively use your preparation (roadmap)?

You then also look over your notes. Do you know what the other party wants? What (they said) their goal is? What their conditions are? Did you check if values that were given are flexible, if they are negotiable? Do you know what is most important for them? Did you listen and observe carefully? Did they give you any information? And how did they respond to your conditions and ambitions?

2. You weigh up/balance your conditions

You are now in a position to weigh up or to balance your conditions. For this, you go through your list of conditions, and for every vital condition, you give your ambition a value of 100 points and your limit a value of 0 points (zero). Without exception, your vital conditions will range from 100 points to 0 points.

For your optional, additional or 'champagne' conditions, you decide on the number of points you wish to attribute to the value of your ambition, based on the relative importance of the condition for you *at this specific time in your life*.

EXAMPLE

Imagine you are negotiating a new job, one that is a fantastic professional opportunity for your career. The location of this job is in the centre of a large city where parking space is scarce and expensive. As you live in a remote location with little access to public transport, you need your car. Therefore you have decided that one of your conditions is having access to a company parking place. This condition is very important to you (i.e. worth 90 points). It is, however, not a vital condition, because not having a company parking place would not make you turn down this great new job opportunity, even if it will make your life more complicated.

No 'champagne' condition has a limit or a 0 value because they are not vital. So, for every 'champagne' condition, you weigh its relative importance and give it a maximum number of points (that can never equal or be more than 100). See the ambition and limits tool below to understand how to weigh up or balance your conditions.

AMBITIONS AND LIMITS: TOOL TO WEIGH CONDITIONS

An empty tool might look like the following table. You first start giving points to your ambitions and filling in your ambition column, and setting to 0 the limits of your vital conditions (and only those). Only once your conditions have been weighed (see the example below) will you be able to fill in the 'reaction of the other party' column.

TABLE 10.1

Conditions	Ambition	Reaction of the other party	Limit
A (first vital condition)			
B (second vital condition)			
C (third vital condition)			
D (first optional condition)			
e (first optional condition)			
f (first optional condition)			
g ...			

An example: I want this great job under certain conditions (UCC).

TABLE 10.2

Conditions	Ambition in points	Reaction of the other party	Limit
A (salary)	100		0
B (holidays)	100		0
C (starting date)	100		0
D (parking place)	90		
e (size of office)	90		
f (home working)	60		
g (choice of computer)	80		
h (having 2 screens)	50		
i (access to a number of training days/year)	80		
...			

3. You position the other party's reaction

For every condition you communicated for which you received a reaction/ response, you estimate its value in points *for you* and then transcribe the answer you got into the space that lies between your ambition and – if there is one – your limit. This does means that you need to have had a reaction on the value you gave, to have listened and if necessary probed for an answer. For instance, when you suggested 13 September 2022 as a starting date of the project, did they say *yes, no, maybe, sooner please*? You decide how many points you feel their answer is worth, once again based on the importance of the condition for you at this moment and write it on your scale. This exercise is important as it allows you to give relative importance to your conditions and enables you to have a clearer view of what you have possibly achieved.

TABLE 10.3

Conditions	Ambition	Reaction zone of the other party	Limit
A (salary)	100 (I asked for £120,000 a year)	80 (they said that £100,000 would be possible)	0
B (holidays)	100 (I wanted 6 weeks)	70 (they said 4 weeks is the norm)	0
C (starting date)	100 (I wanted to start in 6 months)	50 (they said the starting date was in 3 months)	0
D (parking place)	90	none (there is no parking available)	
e (office)	90 (I wanted to be alone)	60 (they said I would need to share 2 days per week)	
f (home working)	60 (I wanted to work from home 2 days a week)	30 (they said ½ day from home could be considered)	
g (choice of computer)	80 (I wanted to be able to have a Mac)	80 (yes, choice possible between Mac and PC)	
h (having 2 screens)	50 (I wanted 2 screens)	50 (yes, required by job)	
i (access to a number of training days/ year)	80 (I wanted to have 10 days training a year)	20 (not in the first year, but after 12 months' employment)	

4. You plan your strategy and compensate

Every time you are given a value that does not match your ambition, i.e. that makes you move away from your best value, ask yourself two questions:

- *Do I want to move away as much as this from my ambition?*
- *And if so, against what – how will I compensate the withdrawal?*

In other words, *There is no capacity for withdrawal without compensation.* This is a fundamental rule: you only accept a movement away from your ambition against a gain on another condition. However, the value of the compensation once again depends only on the importance of the condition for you. On one, you may choose a more symbolic compensation, and on another, you might decide to compensate with several slightly more important ones.

EXAMPLE

In the above example, say the company tells you during your interview that there is no possibility of a parking space. You may then decide that to compensate for this fact, you will try asking for financial help for a public transport pass and to be able to start work in the morning at a time that will allow you to avoid the main rush hour.

Why is compensation so important? For two reasons. First of all, giving creates a system of accountability ('*I owe you something*') and of dependency,[2] building a subtle power/gratitude game. Second, giving does not have the same value as an exchange, simply by virtue of being a gift (if it is given, then it is not worth as much).

Negotiator Laurent Combalbert talks about this in an article on the 'Gilets Jaunes' crisis:

> During the last weeks of 2018, early weeks of 2019, the French government was struggling with the 'Gilets Jaunes' strikers in a lengthy arm-wrestle. One analysis of the situation was critical of the Macron government for conceding a substantial sum of money without ensuring compensation (such as ending the protest demonstrations). What one gives unilaterally (without asking for or receiving) something in exchange) loses all value for the receiving party. The 'Gilets Jaunes', who received this considerable sum, remained dissatisfied... and the crisis continues.[3]

On some conditions you may choose to refuse a large concession. For example, imagine the condition 'work presence in the office'; your ambition may be to be present three days in the office and to work from home for two days. During the interview, the company representatives responded to your wish by stating that they expected 4.5 days in the office. When you are analysing your data to have a good idea of what you have achieved so far and to build a proposal, you may decide that half a day at home is too little, so you will try to get more. Therefore you might state that you would be willing to have four days in the office so long you can keep one fixed day working from home (here you have brought in two conditions: a fixed day at home (i.e. the day is not variable) and the number of days, i.e. one full one).

The fact that you know you will compensate any movement away from your ambitions encourages you to be less tough and rigid: you realize that it is only because you are flexible that you will get something in exchange for your willingness to move away from your best and what you asked for.

The example below illustrates the thought process to decide whether or not to withdraw, and if so how to compensate. For instance, take the first condition, 'salary'. You suggested (your ambition) an annual salary, which for you is worth 100 points. They came with a counter offer, which for you

CONDITION	A	THE OTHER'S REACTION	L	10.3
WORK PRESENCE IN THE OFFICE OR ON SITE	3 DAYS A WEEK	4 OR 5 DAYS A WEEK		

1 Do I accept moving away from my ambition?
2 And if I do, against what? (How will I compensate?)

represents 80 points. If you accept their counter offer, how do you compensate the loss of 20 points? This could be by asking for home working possibilities, or a parking place or a travel card paid by the company, or flexitime. Any condition that for you is worth the relative loss you incur on your vital condition 'salary'. You then go down the entire list checking and compensating.

5. You define your strategy towards the other party's conditions

You then take the notes you have taken concerning the other party, and you ask yourself the same questions for each of their requests:

- Will you give them what they want (in total or in part)?
- And if yes, against what? (The 'what' can take the form of a movement on another one of their conditions – e.g. not giving them as much as they asked for – or you can bring in one of yours).

TABLE 10.4

| MY CONDITIONS | AMBITION | | | | | | REACTION ZONE
Do I move – and if I do, against what? | LIMIT |

	POINTS							
	100	80	60	40	20	0		
A *(SALARY)*	⊙	▲						0
B *(HOLIDAYS)*	⊙		▲					0
C *(START DATE)*	⊙			▲				0
D *(PARKING SPACE)*	⊙							
E *(WORKING SPACE)*	⊙		▲					
f *(SIZE OF OFFICE)*	⊙	▲						
g *(CAFETERIA)*			⊙ ▲					
h *(CHOICE OF COMPUTER)*		⊙			▲			
i *(HAVING TWO SCREENS)*			⊙ ▲					

> **KEY**
>
> ⊙   YOU REQUEST
>
> ▲   THE OTHER'S REACTION

It is important to remember at all times that:

- Building your offer and strategy does not mean you are willing to negotiate. This exercise is not a commitment to negotiation; it is more like a test, a sounding board. You are trying to see *what would happen if you were to go further, if you were to agree to …*

- To negotiate means to accept the principle and dynamics of exchange: you do not give, you exchange, and the value of the exchange is set by each party depending on what is important to them at this specific time (because needs, interests and contexts change and evolve).

- No one outside your team will take part in this analysis or see what and how you decided to exchange and compensate. At times you may have compensated conditions that have no logical connection. It doesn't matter: the other will not bear witness to your thoughts, discussions or decisions.

6. You build your offer: 'If you do this (for me), then I will do this (for you)'

You now copy what you and your team decided during the previous step on to a simple two-column document:

TABLE 10.5

If you do this for me …	Then (and only then) I will do this for you…
xxx	yyy
xxx	yyy
xxx	yyy
xxx	yyy
xxx	yyy
xxx	yyy

In the left column, you will have your conditions revisited (i.e. after your decision to accept to move or not), and in the right column their conditions revisited (i.e. after your decision to accept them or not).

The column layout is important. If you were to change them around, i.e. *'If I do this for you'* first, it tends to imply a *'Then would you do this for me?'* – which is more like conditional questioning. Here you have gone beyond the hypothetical, here you are formulating an offer, which, if accepted, will be binding and to which you will be committed.

This tool is an easy way to professionalize presentation and to clarify your offer – which will then be communicated more easily. It also enables any possible imbalance to be clearly visible: if in one column there are 25 conditions, and in the other 11, one party may feel their demands have not been taken into account and they are being 'had', that something is unfair.

Not all the conditions in your roadmap will have been mentioned during the encounters; it is rare to bring them all in as you should have so many of them. However, every condition that is in your offer must have been discussed. At a minimum you need to be sure that all your vital conditions and hopefully most of your important ones figure in your offer as well as all those the other party talked about. Make sure that you have not brought in a new 'weighty' (possibly expensive) condition. This would be springing a new element on the other party and act like a 'bomb' when you present your offer, creating a surprised or shocked reaction or at worst potentially invalidating the whole negotiation.

7. You then decide: is it in your interest to negotiate?

It is only now that you can take a step back, look at your offer as objectively as possible, and decide *whether it is in your best interest to negotiate or not – do you want to pursue it?*

So far you have spent time defining and analysing your goal. You have spent time meeting the other party and discussing with them. You have analysed whether you think you might come to an agreement. Now that you have brought it all together you decide if it is worth continuing the negotiation or not.

Even if it is rare at this stage for either party to pull out, because most items will have been discussed during the encounters, it can happen that something was forgotten, or – when analysing the situation away from the pressure, when there is less emotion – you may see that in fact you do not want to clinch a deal.

Presenting the offer

Once you have decided that it is in your interest to continue the negotiation, you proceed to present your offer, making sure it is clearly understood that it is only a first one and that it is to be discussed as a starting point. Usually one of the following three situations can happen:

- you present your offer first – which is the option to be preferred

- the other party presents their offer first and it does not match yours
- the other party presents their offer first and it matches yours exactly

You present your offer first[4]

When possible (as this could depend on cultural sensibilities and different personalities, age issues or hierarchical levels) it is usually in your best interest to present your offer first. Throughout this model you are, or you seek to be, the starting point, the reference point for further discussions. Remember the encounters are based on *you* communicating your roadmap, so the proposal discussion should if possible be based on your offer. This strategy is influenced by the anchoring bias, a well-known cognitive bias that describes the common tendency to give too much weight to the first number put forward in a discussion. This first number becomes an 'anchor' and people then tend to adapt their opinion or negotiation based on that first mentioned number. All future figures are discussed and interpreted in relationship to this anchor.[5]

You present your offer globally, making sure that you do not make links between your and their conditions, as there often is not a logical connection between them. In other words, '*If you do this and this and this for me, then I will do this and this and this and this for you*' rather than a 'tit for tat' approach.

EXAMPLE

The head of HR of an international company is talking to a potential new recruit:

'I am pleased that we can meet again. Following our various discussions we are delighted to be able to make you the following offer. If you are willing to relocate to Africa and start the job in three weeks, if you can take the on-board training before you leave, if you can put us in contact with two hydro geologists and brief them on the project for when you are away, then we will ensure that you can have (your requested) two months unpaid leave starting in eight weeks, that you can have access to the local team prior to departure, that you can benefit from 10 days training of your choice per year and we will organize for you to do your background research from Geneva and give you an open-ended contract with seven weeks holiday. How does that sound to you?'

Then you wait for the reaction. Welcome silence. Welcome thinking. Do not start justifying your proposal or fill in space. Unfortunately, the temptation is often to talk too much, justifying and over-explaining. This is not necessary – or if it is it means that you probably have not been clear enough during the various encounters, or that your offer contains new (surprising) elements.

Observe.

Your counterpart may react in one of several ways. If you notice surprise or anger, it could mean that you have included a new important 'bombshell' condition without having talked about it beforehand. Or interpreted something they talked about falsely. Or possibly forgotten or ignored something they asked for. Whatever the reason, it is important to take into account their reaction and to act on it. As discussed in Chapters 6 and 7 on communication, if you notice anger, silence or withdrawal, never take it personally or seek to argue and convince the other. Try patience and curiosity instead, to re-establish trust and safety (in the process and discussion); don't get furious – get curious.

However, as mentioned earlier, an offer should be a reflection of the quality of the various encounters and thus the formalization of what was tentatively discussed, therefore reactions should be quite straightforward and unsurprising.

If you are in a multi-party negotiation it is important to keep in mind several things:

- You need to make sure no one party feels left out, and that you do not create a situation where one party or person can have the impression that two teams are up against the third, the 'two against one' syndrome.

- If you present your offer first you may wish to explain how you will proceed. For example: '*In my position as CEO of this company, I am going to present our offer first to A then to B. Please do not interrupt until the end, when I will take your questions and comments*'. Or: '*I have an offer to make to both of you. Please keep note of your questions and remarks for when you have listened to the global offer.*'

If one party feels left out, they will often become disengaged from the process, and may even step out, become aggressive or block any further agreement. One aggressive party can have a very negative influence on the others – depending how expressive and outgoing they are. Remember, emotions are contagious. Even 'closed' body language can have an influence.

Pay attention to (even slight) indications of discontent, and remember the sign of a good negotiation is sustainability.

The other party presents their offer first and it doesn't match yours

If the other party communicate their offer first:

- Listen to the end without interrupting.
- Never react with a counter-offer.
- Instead use their offer as a starting point and deal with one item at a time, talking about the points that do not match what you had in mind or that surprise you.

If you come up directly with a counter-offer, there will be no clear starting point to the discussion and more likely than not a rather chaotic meeting will take place, as each party tends to talk about what they have put on the table.

The other party presents their offer first and it matches yours exactly

If the other party presents their offer first, and it matches yours exactly, listen to the end, stay silent for a minute or two, and then make your acceptance conditional. You could for example say something along the lines of: '*Well, that is an interesting offer. Let me think – if you could add the cost of printing the documents, then we can accept and sign now.*'

This is not being petty: agreeing straight away can lead the others to think they have been hard done by, that they probably have missed an opportunity, left out something, been 'had' or were misled. When someone says yes directly to an offer, it is an unfortunate but common reaction to think '*I could have asked for more*', '*Oh dear, what did I miss?*', '*What are they hiding?*' Instead of a direct '*Yes,*' formulate a counter-offer on one very small, symbolic condition to see how much you can improve the offer. The negotiation should end with the other saying '*Yes*' to you. As author Josh Doody points out in his article on salary negotiations,[6] once they say '*Yes*' to you, or you run out of things to ask for, then you have finished negotiating.

Working the offer

Having checked understanding and listened to the initial reactions, the same tools that were used during the encounters are used to clarify and work on the offer.

Make sure you always remember that *you need the other party to get this deal under way*. It is extremely powerful to keep this in mind at all times – the other party remains your current best opportunity throughout the process. Except if the situation for some reason degenerates and you decide to stop the discussion and walk out, it is always in your interest to manage your emotions as best you can and to remain calm and analytical. The good news is that usually, when you get to the stage of presenting a formal proposal, the parties know each other because they have had several meetings to discuss and build a more trusting environment. Any possible animosity or misunderstandings should have been talked about and handled before reaching this stage.

Refrain from arguing: you are not here to make your point and convince the other but to clinch a deal, a partnership that will bring all parties something they need. Instead of '*No, that doesn't work for me*' (two negative words) you can say, '*I would be more comfortable with…*' (positive words). Negative words slow things down and tend to put up walls that make collaboration difficult. Using only positive words is difficult at first, but gets easier with practice.

Avoid insisting and continuously coming back to a blocking point; seek rather to use new ideas and assumptions to move forward. Tackle difficult points as soon as possible and use hypothetical questions to unblock the situation. Remain open to new ways of seeing things and consciously (i.e. do not simply assume they know it) show your flexibility. Always think in terms of 'exchange' and not 'gift'. Unsolicited generosity always finishes by creating obligations where one feels trapped in a labyrinth of dependency.

Finalizing the offer and clinching the deal

Eventually, the important points will have all been discussed and you realize you are coming towards a negotiated agreement that is acceptable to all parties. When this happens you might choose to check that you can move on to clinch the deal, for instance by saying, '*It seems to me that we have covered all the points that have been discussed. If you agree with this shall we move forward?*'

However enthusiastic or relieved you might feel, or even simply worn out by the exercise, it is important that you concentrate until the end. As the saying goes, the devil is in the detail… Show overall acceptance only when all points are crystal clear, agreed on and accepted, and make sure you do not leave room for interpretation – remember that everything you write and say will be binding.

Usually the implementation terms will have been discussed during the final encounters and you will need to arrange a meeting to review the situation and implementation of the agreed points (see Chapter 11). Special care will need to be maintained until the end as all interested partners and parties must sign the agreement.

Final check

It is always advisable to make a final check with the involved parties, asking them how they feel about the agreement and in fact the entire process and finding out their satisfaction level with the negotiated deal. There are two ways you can do this.

Once the agreement has been signed – and only then – ask the other party/parties if they are satisfied with the deal, or ask them how they feel. If the process has been run as described in this model, most often the answer will be 'Good', 'Satisfied'. If, however, there was a hidden agenda, or an unexpressed need, or if one personality type overruled the meetings and one party couldn't express certain issues, then the answer may be 'Good but', 'Fine but'. In this case it is important to take note of the 'but', to acknowledge it. Never ignore any sign of potential dissatisfaction or frustration; take it into account. For example you could react in the following way: 'I regret this was not mentioned earlier, but here is what I suggest: we move forward as planned, and in three months we schedule a meeting to discuss the point you have just brought up. How does that sound?'

If a 'Yes but' is ignored, there is a possibility that the concerned party will block or hinder implementation of the negotiated agreement, either actively or passively. This can have consequences on the actual deal and should be avoided – you do not want to have wasted such precious time and effort. If, however, a 'Yes but' is acknowledged and a promise is made to at least discuss it and see what can be done – in all honesty – then you face a better chance that the frustrated party will engage in the agreement until their point is on the agenda. Often the point that has been raised becomes a condition for the other party. At times it might feel uncomfortable to ask – particularly if you are not sure that the other party is getting an interesting deal – but it is important to do so, in your own words. A great deal, if not put into practice and respected, is at best a waste of time.

Another way to query satisfaction level is to use a solution-focused scaling question on the confidence level of each party in the successful implementation of the agreement. Your question would look like:

> '*On a scale from 1 to 10, where 10 means you are totally confident and 1 means you have no confidence at all, how confident do you feel that this agreement will be put into practice?*'

If the answer is a low figure you might react by asking '*What would it take for you to give a slightly higher number?*' or '*What would be different if you were one step higher on the scale?*' You then need to work with the answer, either directly if the issue is straightforward or as above, at a later date, with the point that has been raised becoming a condition for the other party.

Chapter 10: summary points

- Negotiation is an iterative process – it may be that you will have to work on several offers before you reach one that is satisfactory to all parties.
- The offer is built on the logic of exchange: there is no capacity for withdrawal without some sort of compensation, even if only a symbolic one. Each and every movement away from your ambition needs to be compensated with another condition or with movement on an existing condition.
- Each change, reaction, request made to a condition is evaluated: is it acceptable or not, and if yes, against what.
- Your reality determines the value of the exchange: it is the interest the condition holds for you rather than its 'market value' which is most important. The elements that are exchanged do not necessarily have the same value.
- The cement of the relationship remains the interests of all parties. These must be met at least in part, even if the interests differ.
- There should be no room for interpretation: everything must be very precise and clearly understood.
- Concentrate until the end – the devil is in the detail.
- Throughout this step, social intuition and communication skills (as discussed in Chapters 6, 7 and 9) are of the utmost importance.
- All the parties need to agree, engage and sign the agreement.

Notes

1   M Durickas. Quote of the day: If you're walking down the right path and you're willing to keep walking, eventually you'll make progress, Contemporaries, 2019. www.bostoncontemporaries.com/2019/03/01/quote-of-the-day-if-youre-walking-down-the-right-path-and-youre-willing-to-keep-walking-eventually-youll-make-progress/ (archived at https://perma.cc/AB49-FLDE)

2   *The Economist*, A paradox at the heart of gift-giving, 2018. www.economist.com/science-and-technology/2018/06/28/a-paradox-at-the-heart-of-gift-giving (archived at https://perma.cc/8WRY-37F5)

3   L Combalbert. *Le Point*, 17 January 2019, n 2420, 51

4   Science Daily. Anchoring bias in decision-making. www.sciencedaily.com/terms/anchoring.htm (archived at https://perma.cc/MMG7-3LKT) and K Shonk. What is anchoring in negotiation? Harvard Law School, 2021. www.pon.harvard.edu/daily/negotiation-skills-daily/what-is-anchoring-in-negotiation/ (archived at https://perma.cc/ZEF4-W2R9)

5   Science Daily. Anchoring bias in decision-making. www.sciencedaily.com/terms/anchoring.htm (archived at https://perma.cc/MMG7-3LKT) and K Shonk. What is anchoring in negotiation? Harvard Law School, 2021. www.pon.harvard.edu/daily/negotiation-skills-daily/what-is-anchoring-in-negotiation/ (archived at https://perma.cc/ZEF4-W2R9)

6   J Doody. Never, ever utter these phrases in a salary negotiation, Fast Company, 2018. www.fastcompany.com/90246630/what-not-to-say-in-a-salary-negotiation (archived at https://perma.cc/55QQ-KE82)

11

Step 5: the implementation

The final step of the negotiation process concerns the implementation of the negotiated agreement. This chapter will take you through some best practice requirements related to the agreement in action and to how what has been negotiated will actually be carried out and implemented. It will clarify some of the fundamental requirements to take into account to ensure that what has been agreed to between you and your counterparts is effectively put into practice. Most of these elements will in fact have been translated into conditions that were negotiated during the final encounters and will be included in the main deal. Milestones and responsibilities will need to be determined. Some simple project management tools will help with this step.

Implementing the negotiated decision

There is always a risk that what has been discussed and negotiated remains 'in the drawer' and that the decisions that have been taken are never put into practice. Usually this only happens when one or more of the parties involved lose interest in the process. The aim of this last step in the negotiation process – the implementation – is to make sure that the negotiated decisions are in fact carried out. It is about the agreement going live and the partnership being sustained. This final step may be the shortest and simplest one to describe, but it remains as important as the previous ones as it finalizes the entire process.

A common error is to actually forget to discuss and decide how the agreement will be implemented, which can lead to many decisions remaining in the realms of good intentions and wishful thinking, or worse neglected, gathering dust in drawers. Not implementing plans is a waste of time for all parties, and – far worse still – can hinder further attempts to negotiate with the same people. Ideally, aspects pertaining to the 'go live' have been talked about during the final encounters, so, during the previous step (the offer), it is important to have thought about what it would take for the negotiated agreement to become a reality, and to make sure what has been decided is clearly stated in the proposal and agreed on.

Depending on the complexity of the negotiation and on the number of parties involved, one person or a small team need to be appointed with the responsibility for the implementation of the agreement. Their skills should involve high communication, organizational, project management and negotiation competences as well as charisma and determination. Their roles, which will have to be clarified, agreed on and communicated, might vary from coordinating to acting as experts or to actually carrying out what has been decided. If many parties are involved, the team should be made up of a representative of each. At times it might be useful to take on board someone independent and neutral for overseeing the implementation; however, the more the parties concerned in the actual outcome are involved in the process, the smoother the implementation will be. When a team is motivated by an outcome, it will be easier to handle those hurdles that are bound to occur. Remember, as mentioned in the beginning of this book, the main indicator of the success of a negotiation is whether what has been negotiated is put into practice, and whether the agreement is binding and endures.

The final negotiated agreement will thus contain decisions pertaining to action plans, follow-up points, responsibilities and deadlines. This entire step bears strong similarities to elements of project management and coordination. It can help to break down the goal into smaller sub-goals. With each step forward, you thus feel as though you are advancing toward future successes. Academic research based on animal behaviour has shown that people are more motivated, and tend to move faster, when the end is in sight. This phenomenon is known as the goal gradient.[1] Situational monitoring must be carefully and regularly carried out. Due to changing circumstances – whether organizational, political or economic – some (parts of) negotiated agreements become obsolete, less relevant or undesirable over time. Katie Shonk in her article on the Starbucks–Kraft dispute advises that cancellation clauses and compensation conditions for ending agreements early should be planned for.[2] It is also important for all stakeholders' continued motivation to point out and make sure to take stock of what has been achieved, especially when you're just starting out. Measuring early progress at the beginning can be as motivating as using a goal that's in sight at the end to spur you to the finish line.[3]

The following recommendations should be observed to ensure an implementation that is as smooth and efficient as possible.

First of all you need to remain vigilant for any change in circumstances, whether external (such as geo-political) or internal (for example within an organization or a team). For instance, within company X there is a sudden departmental reorganization that renders the agreement between two entities unnecessary as they have been merged, or the activities of one has been outsourced; or the negotiations concern a country in which the leader of a rebel group has been killed and the rebel group disbanded, thus rendering the negotiations void; or a natural catastrophe or pandemic has changed government priorities; a new law has been voted; Brexit has happened, a new president and political party has been voted in...

You need to remain aware throughout of anything that might affect the negotiated agreement or partnership and (seek to) adapt accordingly.

Another point that needs to be kept in mind at all times is the importance of maintaining the ongoing interest of all involved parties, being very attentive to them and keeping check throughout. For the partnership to be put in action, the interest of all must continue for the agreement to be respected and for the right momentum to be maintained.

As with more traditional project management, to help implementation and momentum, break big projects into smaller tasks, because as data has pointed out in psychologist Ayelet Fishbach's research on setting goals,[4] 'motivation waxes and wanes as you work on a particular goal. You start off motivated, and you are motivated again towards the end of a project. But in the middle stretch, your motivation tends to lag'. Therefore, it is advisable to break down the agreement into a series of 'quick wins' or smaller steps to:

- Show all stakeholders that *it is possible*.

- Sustain interest and engagement, if possible even enthusiasm, so as to keep momentum and energy.

- Ensure something is actually being done – and make sure that the various parties are aware of this fact. Communication is important so that everyone knows what is happening.

Another element that is found in traditional project management is the need to carefully decide with all the stakeholders:

- responsibilities and tasks: who is responsible for doing what?
- deadlines: by when?
- tools and methods: how should it be done?
- resources: with what means?

You will also need to prepare and agree to an implementation budget (for instance to cover travel expenses if meetings are to be held in physical presence, to pay for legal fees for writing up contracts, to name an external consultant to coordinate the implementation plan...).

Finally, several status and review meetings will need to be planned in advance to ensure all stakeholders are present and involved in the actual process of bringing the agreement to life.

Chapter 11: summary points

- It is advisable that the implementation points are discussed during the (final) encounters and that they are negotiated with the agreement. They thus become negotiated conditions.

- Regular review meetings will need to be organized to follow up on agreed points. Good project management skills are of great benefit for ensuring implementation, coordination and follow-up.

- Be very aware and highly vigilant about any changes of circumstances and adapt the agreement accordingly. Political, organizational, social and personal circumstances change constantly. What was true today may well not be true tomorrow. This is particularly the case for long-winded negotiations. The eventuality and possibility for adapting the negotiated agreement when necessary must be taken into account and planned for.

- Make sure you carefully plan for adequate communication to all the parties involved in the negotiation and in the implementation of the agreement: a communication strategy will be useful.

- Always keep in mind that clarity and transparency, integrity and respect all contribute to sustainable partnerships and lasting relationships, and to the agreement being honoured.

- At all times, remember that interest remains key to the end.

- A successful negotiation is one in which what has been negotiated is actually put into practice. As seen in Chapter 1, it is not only the quality of the content that characterizes success, it is also the efficient implementation.

Notes

1 'This insight comes originally from academic research into animal behaviour, including studies of rats in a maze,' says Chicago Booth's Oleg Urminsky. 'Proximity to the goal increases motivation. If you're a rat in a maze, you run faster the closer you get to the end." AG Walton. What happened to your goals? Chicago Booth Review, 2017. https://review.chicagobooth.edu/behavioral-science/2017/article/what-happened-your-goals (archived at https://perma.cc/7PHT-X7V6)

2 K Shonk. Negotiation in business: Starbucks and Kraft's coffee conflict – What happens to a negotiated business agreement when it becomes undesirable over time, Harvard Law School, 2018. www.pon.harvard.edu/daily/business-negotiations/the-starbucks-kraft-dispute-in-business-negotiations-prepare-for-problems/ (archived at https://perma.cc/375A-5E7E)

3 A G Walton. What happened to your goals? Chicago Booth Review, 2017. https://review.chicagobooth.edu/behavioral-science/2017/article/what-happened-your-goals?source=ic-em- (archived at https://perma.cc/L5LQ-WSEE)

4 Yale School of Management. Prof Ayelet Fishbach on maintaining motivation and achieving your goals, 2019. https://som.yale.edu/event/2019/02/how-to-achieve-your-goals-insights-from-the-behavioral-science-with-ayelet-fishbach-visiting-professor-of-behavioral-science-and-marketing (archived at https://perma.cc/TC93-X58A)

PART FIVE

Gender

12

A few thoughts on gender and negotiation skills

This chapter shares some insights on the influence of gender on negotiation encounters, behaviours and outcomes. The word gender is used to describe the characteristics of women and men that are socially constructed, whilst sex refers to those that are biologically determined.[1] Nowadays, gender refers to a range of identities that are not necessarily limited to male and female. To avoid confusion, in the following chapter the main gender categories that will be discussed are linked with male and female negotiators.

Are there significant differences in the way women and men negotiate? And if so, do these differences show in the results of the negotiations? Some – at times subtle – differences in the way men and women negotiate have been observed and researched in some parts of the world. What are these gender differences? How have they influenced negotiation attitudes and techniques? Do they have a greater or lesser impact than personality traits on how you behave and are perceived?

These questions will find some answers in the first part of this chapter. The next part will focus on stereotypes and on how they influence behaviour. Stereotypes do exist and whilst these perceived notions may be false they still can impact negotiations. It is also possible and even quite common for someone to confine themselves to a limiting stereotype, which will often have an adverse effect on their communication and negotiation style, and at times on their willingness to actually engage in a negotiation. The next section introduces the notion of gender backlash, and is followed by some thoughts and considerations on how race and culture impact gender differences in negotiation behaviour. Finally, with over 25 years' experience as a female negotiator, I will share some personal thoughts and insights on the subject.

Gender stereotypes in negotiation behaviour: myth or reality?

The way you view yourself will influence how you behave and interact, and thus will have an impact on how others behave and respond back. As Katie Byron wrote, a thought is harmless unless one believes in it, and, unfortunately, those thoughts that are most firmly believed are rarely the most helpful or encouraging ones.[2] These can include '*I am not good enough*', '*In any case I will never manage…*', '*Nobody will listen to me because I am…*'.

Do you believe you are less able to negotiate because you are a woman? Or because you are a man? Or are the differences linked more with personality than gender? Or possibly a mix of both?

What one focuses on helps shape one's reality. To paraphrase Richard Bach, author of *Jonathan Livingston Seagull*,[3] if you argue for your limitation, then sure enough they become your limitations.

Different behaviours exist.

Stereotypes exist.

Stereotypes are traditionally defined as over-generalized attributes that are associated with the members of a social group, such as the reserved English or the geeky engineer, with the implication that it applies to all group members.[4] These mental pictures often represent an oversimplified, prejudiced attitude. And, whether they are based on fact or on a social construct, gender stereotypes exist and can affect behaviour when negotiating.

Stereotype threat exists.

The theory of stereotype threat posits that stigmatized group members may underperform on diagnostic tests of ability through concerns about confirming a negative societal stereotype as self-characteristic.[5] In other words, if someone knows that there is a stereotype about the group they belong to, the chances that they act out of that stereotype are higher than if they did not realize there was a stereotype about that group.[6]

Stereotypes are incredibly powerful constructs that influence how people behave and interact. In fact stereotypes influence a person's entire worldview, whether consciously or not. Toosi *et al* explain that gender stereotypes impact negotiation behaviour by providing mental schemas of how those who identify with a particular gender would and should behave before and during the negotiation.[7] Some of the stereotypes often linked with women and negotiations are the beliefs and thoughts such as '*women are bad negotiators*', '*women are less assertive*', '*women are more accommodating*', '*women are more emotional*', '*women ask for less*' can unconsciously cause a negatively biased outcome for women, downplaying their capabilities. A woman being too assertive or a man being too kind will be criticized. Whatever you do you will be criticized. Should this stop you trying? In my view, no. Being aware of this will, however, help, because it will enable you to adapt your behaviour and negotiation strategy.

Some of the stereotypes that are often associated with women negotiators include being (too) kind, cooperative, rarely assertive, downplaying themselves and what they want, being stronger on emotional intelligence skills, putting more focus on the relationship than on the outcome, and generally being more empathetic than their masculine counterparts. However, often what is written and said about gender stereotypes is over simplified. It is probably more useful and accurate to consider gender as a fluid and socially constructed category that is highly impacted by culture rather than a fixed and rigid set of characteristics tied to biological sex.[8]

And yet it has been observed that women who adopt a more assertive stance will often generate strong reactions, particularly when they focus solely on their own goals and purpose.

Gender backlash

Woman backlash is a phenomenon whereby some people have a negative reaction against women – in fact this could happen with any gender minority – whose behaviours violate the gender norms of that culture.

When talking about women negotiators, for instance, it has been noted that *in most but not all cultures* (see page 183) assertive self-advocating women who put forward their interests can suffer negative social judgements (i.e. backlash) because their behaviour is associated with high negative masculine and low positive feminine characteristics. These women are believed to be competent but unlikeable.[9]

Backlash is not only directed towards women. Toosi *et al* noted that low-status individuals are often punished for behaving in ways that are reserved for high-status individuals. If low-status people negotiate assertively in an individualistic society, they are likely to receive backlash.[10] It could be assumed that the same applies for all minority groups. The researchers do however point out that levels of backlash against assertive female negotiators has been inferred but not formally tested.

Because they are scared of or wary about backlash and stereotype threat,[11] many women are less likely to engage in assertive negotiation behaviour because they fear negative judgements related to being unlikeable.[12]

Should the fear of – real or perceived – backlash stop a woman, or even anyone, from negotiating? Whether man or woman, fear of negative consequences, although at times a possibly sensible move, is most often the best way to fail to achieve your goal by not even trying or by giving up too soon.

What women focus on impacts their counterparts' reactions and the negotiated outcomes. A number of studies on gender differences in negotiation behaviours have pointed out that when the result of the negotiation is oriented to the collective good (team, community, family), women negotiated better than when the result is aimed at self-fulfilment. Toosi *et al* note that women negotiate just as effectively as men when they are doing so on behalf of others.[13] In other words, when negotiating on behalf of another individual, group or community, women are more assertive (similar in style to male negotiators) and successful (reaping similar financial benefits for the person they are advocating for). Furthermore, assertive women advocating for others confirm gender role expectations of being supportive and nurturing, while assertive women who advocate for themselves violate these gender role expectations. These findings are, however, still inherently rooted in Western cultural values.

Coming back to the five step negotiation process that is described in this handbook, an important way to help frame the negotiation in terms of benefits to others and advocacy is through the linkage tool. As discussed in Chapter 3, the upper part of the linkage tool focuses on values and motivations. Values and many motivating factors are linked with the self, however there will almost always be some that can be related to others – whether 'others' refers to the team, the organization, the group, nature, your family, the 'common good', etc.

Advocacy, awareness of why you want what you want and clarity of volition are all important elements to a successful negotiation and will encourage more assertive and self-confident negotiation behaviours. In self-oriented negotiations – i.e. a negotiation that focuses only on gaining something for oneself – it may be helpful to make a concerted effort at reframing the negotiation goal into a more 'other-oriented' exchange so that some of the benefits will also be helpful to others and the 'greater good'.

How culture and race influence gender bias

Toosi *et al* analysed the extent to which gender norms are in fact highly culturally dependent.[14] They point out that most research on gender bias in negotiations has focused on predominantly Western cultures and has neglected several other important aspects, namely that ethnicity and culture should also be taken into account when looking at gender influence on negotiation outcomes. They suggest that the underlying assumption that men are stereotyped as agentic[15] and women are stereotyped as communal is conditioned by the cultural values and practices of the society and is not a universal phenomenon. For instance, in collectivist societies such as China and Korea, men are more likely to be stereotyped as communal – with relationship-oriented negotiating behaviours – and women as agentic, which represents the opposite pattern found in individualistic cultures found in the West.[16] Attributing differences in negotiating behaviour solely to gender alone simplifies a more complex pattern. Awareness and understanding of the interactions between ethnicity and gender with culture give instead a more comprehensive insight into negotiation behaviours. They conclude that:

- Cultural values and practices guide negotiation behaviour throughout the negotiation process.

- Negotiation behaviour will be different for men and women, reflecting gender stereotypes that encourage men and women to behave differently. Cultural norms and values will dictate what is expected as the appropriate or correct behaviour for the dominant category, which, in terms of gender, is most often men.

- Despite cultural differences in how men and women negotiate, the immediate economic impact of negotiating behaviour on negotiation outcomes is consistent across societies.

Personal thoughts and experience

How can a woman turn 'femininity' into a positive advantage? I do not mean using one's charms or physical attributes. Rather I mean that someone may feel less threatened by a woman and this in itself is an interesting advantage. According to Professor Laurie Weingart, being more accommodating and collaborative is without doubt useful for sustainable and lasting negotiations.[17]

I have been asked on numerous occasions whether I believe there is a difference in negotiation styles and negotiated outcomes between men and women. This is a challenging question. I have been a professional negotiator for over 25 years and I am a woman. Does the fact that I am a woman help or hinder my negotiation capabilities, or influence them in any way?

There are probably real differences between the way men and women negotiate and their respective communication styles. More importantly, I believe that to enclose oneself in an image or a stereotype is akin to imprisoning oneself in an often negative self-fulfilling prophecy, and as such is to be avoided at all costs. Both men and women have traits and skills that can be useful in a negotiation, and it is those skills that are to be built upon and developed.

Thus my personal experience and instinct clamour that successful negotiations are not gender-dependent, even though the fact that I am a woman most probably has an influence on the way others perceive me and the way I perceive myself. This would be the same if I were small, large, not European, beautiful or plain. People will automatically react to and be influenced by the external signs they perceive. Indeed, people are fine-tuned to sense, react and jump to conclusions.

My belief is that differences in personality and in behaviour will influence both the negotiation outcome and the dynamics of the encounters more than differences in gender. During the many negotiations I have been involved in, whether real ones or case studies, I have witnessed time and time again that personality traits make the biggest difference. Take for instance the personality traits introversion and extroversion that have been widely researched. It is often assumed that extroverts—those who tend to be more outgoing and draw their energy from others—are better negotiators than introverts, who generally are more reserved and prefer to think things through on their own. Indeed, more outgoing people may benefit in negotiations from their ability to bring people together and respond quickly and skilfully to others' emotions. However, many of the strengths of someone with a more introvert personality are highly beneficial in negotiation, including their tendency to listen closely without interruption and to take more time to think. These personality traits are not gender dependent: both men and women can have introvert or extrovert tendencies. Clearly, as Susan Cain analyses in her book *Quiet*, introverts and extroverts can learn a great deal from each other and both can be valuable around a negotiation table.[18]

Make no mistake: I am not ignoring or belittling the fact that women are often treated differently from men in negotiations. If we take a look at both sides of the negotiation table, we find that often women negotiate differently from men and, even when they negotiate in a similar way their acts are perceived differently. Linda C Babcock, in her book *Women Don't Ask*, points out that women therefore may require a more 'calibrated' approach, which doesn't mean that they should not negotiate, but rather that they need to be more strategic about it.[19]

I will, however, make the hypothesis that, for instance, the same can be said of a person of a particular ethnic background amongst a group that is predominantly of a different ethnicity, or a teenager amongst a group of adults. Minorities have it harder. As Michelle Obama, former USA First Lady and author, argues, her husband Barack would be intensely scrutinized at all times because he was a black candidate, and that as such he could not afford any mistake or stumble. She further talks about the fact that he would always have to do everything twice as well, and about the constant pressure to (over) perform.[20] Many women feel much the same: they need to outperform to ensure success.

We adopt different behaviours, sometimes for innate reasons and sometimes due to our own beliefs. I am deeply convinced of the negative power of stereotype threat, 'which has been argued to show a reduction in the performance of individuals who belong to negatively stereotyped groups,'[21] becoming anxious about their performance and thus hindering their ability to perform to their full potential. Any person belonging to a minority group will understand the danger of the stereotypes linked to the group to which they belong, be it gender, ethnicity, age or other. Women who do not negotiate may refrain because they are shy. Or because they may, instead, be anticipating very real attitudes and very real reactions that are borne out, time and again, in real life. However real these are, warns Linda Babcock, women should be aware of but not imprisoned by such findings, and should negotiate for what they want and believe, regardless of the stereotypes those tactics might contradict.[22]

Negotiation is a skill, a mindset and a set of tools that can be learned, *and which apply for all genders*. What contributes to being an outstanding negotiator is more linked to personality and competences than to gender. Do I listen more carefully because I am a woman or because of my personality? And does it really matter as long as I do listen carefully? Social intuition influences negotiation outcomes – is social intuition linked with personality or practice or gender?

In my workshops and during my professional negotiations, my aim is to get away from stereotypical beliefs, because I find them to be diminishing and reductive. Although it is important to talk about stereotypes and to be aware of them, the more we voice them, the more chance there is of stereotype threat acting because we are influenced by what we hear. Whilst there are traits that tend to be found more in the female or male populations, all traits appear in each gender; in order to go beyond stereotypes, this is the message that we need to convey to both women and men. Differences in behaviour can often be better explained by differences in personality than differences in gender, and the same is true for negotiators.

My recommendations are twofold. First of all it is important to be aware of how stereotype threats and fear of backlash influence negotiation behaviour. Second, skills are developed and practised. Avoid thinking you are not good at it, and keep trying. In summary, as Fatimah Gilliam, founder and CEO of The Azara Group, claims, becoming a good negotiator takes as much practice as being a top sportsperson or great musician.[23] In other words, even if some people are naturally better than others, you need to work at it to improve and succeed.

Chapter 12: summary points

- Gender stereotypes that place women negotiators at a disadvantage compared to men should not be universally applied to all women or all men. Ethnicity, culture, gender and personality are all tightly connected and impact the way people negotiate.

- Negotiation is a skill that can be learned, where the same rules apply for all genders. When comparing men and women negotiators, when untrained, men tend to fare better. However, when women have followed skills training they tend to fare as well as if not better than their masculine counterparts.

- Putting more emphasis on the relationship as an important outcome of negotiation is of primary importance to the sustainability of negotiated agreement. This undermines gender stereotypes about negotiation whereby women don't get as good results as men do, as both the content *and* the relationship are important.

- An oversimplified view of being masculine or feminine without considering culture and context leads to inappropriate stereotyping. Social status, cultural norms and social expectations in conjunction with intersections of race and gender shape negotiation behaviours and outcome.

- It is completely expected and even acceptable for women to behave competitively and focus on their own interests in negotiation contexts, depending on the geographical region and culture of the racial majority.

- Women can be highly competent and likeable negotiators. Highly developed social intuition (see Chapter 9) will enable them to be assertive whilst adopting behaviour and attitudes that are considered firm and fair.

- Successful negotiations in terms of content and sustainability depend more on skills than on gender.

- Focus on your negotiation and desired outcome, and not on your gender, even though being aware of perceptions and stereotypes linked to your gender may enhance your social intuition skills.

- It would seem that differences in personality and in behaviour will influence both the negotiation outcome and the dynamics of the encounters more than differences in gender.

Notes

1   World Health Organization. Gender: definitions. www.euro.who.int/en/ health-topics/health-determinants/gender/gender-definitions (archived at https://perma.cc/FFP2-759X)

2   B Katie (2019) *The Work of Byron Katie*, Byron Katie International, Ojai, CA. http://thework.com/wp-content/uploads/2019/02/English_LB.pdf (archived at https://perma.cc/ZD4Y-6XEL)

3   R Bach (1970) *Jonathan Livingston Seagull: A story*, Macmillan, New York

4   P Hinton. Implicit stereotypes and the predictive brain: Cognition and culture in 'biased' person perception, Nature, 2017. www.nature.com/articles/ palcomms201786 (archived at https://perma.cc/7DLH-2ZXJ)

5   C R Pennington, D Heim, A R Ley and D T Larkin. Twenty years of stereotype threat research: A review of psychological mediators, *PLoS One*, 2016, 11 (1). www.ncbi.nlm.nih.gov/pmc/articles/PMC4713435/ (archived at https://perma. cc/WW6U-KZJU)

6   'Stereotype threat is a situational predicament in which people are or feel themselves to be at risk of conforming to stereotypes about their social group'. Wikipedia. Stereotype threat. https://en.wikipedia.org/wiki/Stereotype_ threat#cite_note-6 (archived at https://perma.cc/ET8H-7T87)

7   N R Toosi, Z Semnani-Azad, W Shen, S Mor and E T Amanatullah (2020) How culture and race shape gender dynamics in negotiations, in *Research Handbook on Gender and Negotiation*, ed M Olekalns and J A Kennedy,

Edward Elgar, Cheltenham. www.researchgate.net/publication/340249117_
How_Culture_and_Race_Shape_Gender_Dynamics_in_Negotiations (archived
at https://perma.cc/WCH3-P843)

8 N R Toosi, Z Semnani-Azad, W Shen, S Mor and E T Amanatullah (2020)
How culture and race shape gender dynamics in negotiations, in *Research
Handbook on Gender and Negotiation*, ed M Olekalns and J A Kennedy,
Edward Elgar, Cheltenham. www.researchgate.net/publication/340249117_
How_Culture_and_Race_Shape_Gender_Dynamics_in_Negotiations (archived
at https://perma.cc/WCH3-P843)

9 L A Rudman and J E Phelan. Backlash effects for disconfirming gender
stereotypes in organizations, *Research in Organizational Behavior*, 2008, 28,
61–79

10 E T Amanatullah and C H Tinsley. Punishing female negotiators for asserting
too much… or not enough: Exploring why advocacy moderates backlash
against assertive female negotiators, *Organizational Behavior and Human
Decision Processes*, 2013, 120 (1), 110–22

11 'Stereotype threat is a situational predicament in which people are or feel
themselves to be at risk of conforming to stereotypes about their social group'.
Wikipedia. Stereotype threat. https://en.wikipedia.org/wiki/Stereotype_
threat#cite_note-6 (archived at https://perma.cc/ET8H-7T87)

12 E T Amanatullah and M W Morris. Negotiating gender roles: Gender
differences in assertive negotiating are mediated by women's fear of backlash
and attenuated when negotiating on behalf of others, *Journal of Personality
and Social Psychology*, 2010, 98 (2), 256–67; and HR Bowles, L Babcock and
L Lai. Social incentives for gender differences in the propensity to initiate
negotiations: Sometimes it does hurt to ask, *Organizational Behavior and
Human Decision Processes*, 2007, 103 (1), 84–103, quoted in L A Rudman
and J E Phelan. Backlash effects for disconfirming gender stereotypes in
organizations, *Research in Organizational Behavior*, 2008, 28, 61–79

13 N R Toosi, Z Semnani-Azad, W Shen, S Mor and E T Amanatullah (2020)
How culture and race shape gender dynamics in negotiations, in *Research
Handbook on Gender and Negotiation*, ed M Olekalns and J A Kennedy,
Edward Elgar, Cheltenham. www.researchgate.net/publication/340249117_
How_Culture_and_Race_Shape_Gender_Dynamics_in_Negotiations (archived
at https://perma.cc/WCH3-P843)

14 N R Toosi, Z Semnani-Azad, W Shen, S Mor and E T Amanatullah (2020)
How culture and race shape gender dynamics in negotiations, in *Research
Handbook on Gender and Negotiation*, ed M Olekalns and J A Kennedy,
Edward Elgar, Cheltenham. www.researchgate.net/publication/340249117_
How_Culture_and_Race_Shape_Gender_Dynamics_in_Negotiations (archived
at https://perma.cc/WCH3-P843)

15 The word agentic is described as an individual's power to control his or her own goals, actions and destiny. It stems from the word agency, which Webster's Dictionary defines as the capacity, condition, or state of acting or of exerting power. Merriam-Webster. Agency. www.merriam-webster.com/dictionary/agency (archived at https://perma.cc/5WGW-XXW7)

16 A J C Cuddy, E B Wolf, P Glick, S Crotty, J Chong and M I Norton. Men as cultural ideals: Cultural values moderate gender stereotype content, *Journal of Personality and Social Psychology*, 2015, 109 (4), 622–635, and W Shan, J Keller and L Imai. What's a masculine negotiator? What's a feminine negotiator? It depends on the cultural and situational contexts, *Negotiation and Conflict Management Research*, 2016, 9, 22–43, quoted in N R Toosi, Z Semnani-Azad, W Shen, S Mor and E T Amanatullah (2020) How culture and race shape gender dynamics in negotiations, in *Research Handbook on Gender and Negotiation*, ed M Olekalns and J A Kennedy, Edward Elgar, Cheltenham. www.researchgate.net/publication/340249117_How_Culture_and_Race_Shape_Gender_Dynamics_in_Negotiations (archived at https://perma.cc/WCH3-P843)

17 According to Professor Laurie Weingart there are four basic negotiator personality types: individualists, co-operators, competitives and altruists. Most research suggests that negotiators with a primarily cooperative style are more successful than hard bargainers at reaching novel solutions that improve everyone's outcomes. Negotiators who lean toward cooperation also tend to be more satisfied with the process and their results. And both men and women can be cooperator types, although again women tend to be more associated with such type. K Shonk. Understanding different negotiation styles, Harvard Law School, 2021. www.pon.harvard.edu/daily/negotiation-skills-daily/understanding-different-negotiation-styles/ (archived at https://perma.cc/9FYH-JUF6)

18 S Cain (2013) *Quiet: The power of introverts in a world that can't stop talking*, Broadway Books, New York

19 L Babcock and S Laschever (2003) *Women Don't Ask: The high cost of avoiding negotiation – and positive strategies for change*, Princeton University Press, Princeton, NJ

20 M Obama (2018) *Becoming*, Penguin Books Ltd, New York

21 Wikipedia. Stereotype threat. https://en.wikipedia.org/wiki/Stereotype_threat#cite_note-6 (archived at https://perma.cc/ET8H-7T87)

22 L Babcock and S Laschever (2003) *Women Don't Ask: The high cost of avoiding negotiation – and positive strategies for change*, Princeton University Press, Princeton, NJ

23 Knowledge@Wharton. Women and negotiation: Are there really gender differences? 2015. https://knowledge.wharton.upenn.edu/article/women-and-negotiation-are-there-really-gender-differences (archived at https://perma.cc/JW9Q-8DDA)

Conclusion

Stand out as an excellent negotiator

Whether in complex multi-party negotiations or in more straightforward ones, some people manage to negotiate better and conclude more lasting agreements than others. And some build for themselves a respected reputation along the way. Whilst personality plays an important role, a solid systematic process with specific tools will help anyone improve their skills and therefore the probability of a good and satisfying outcome. Learning the skills and tools and having insight into the process are important. People who have been trained in negotiation skills fare better than people who rely on instinct only.

I believe that what differentiates an average from an excellent negotiation can be summarized by two things:

- **Very thorough preparation** of your roadmap and the motivations behind wanting the goal.
- **A combination of excellent listening skills and social intuition.** As Goethe claimed, 'talking is a necessity, listening is an art', and unless you understand the other party you will not clinch a deal.

It is important to start from the self and then to reach out to the other party, to stay fully and deeply aware throughout the entire negotiation that the other party is your best opportunity *at this moment in time*, to remember at all times that you need them to reach an agreement. Whatever the situation, if you are negotiating it is because you know (possibly had no other choice) that trying together was better than going it alone.

Experienced negotiators such as Lieutenant Jack Cambria of the New York Police Department's hostage negotiation team highlight characteristics that can be applied equally to hostage or business negotiations. Cambria states that the best negotiators are those with life stories. He talks about the importance of knowing how to deal with emotions in a highly charged situation, together with rational decision-making. He strongly advocates the need to listen to learn, instead of entering into a debate. He suggests that negotiators be thoroughly trained in listening skills, believing that in their negotiations virtually all could benefit from spending more time listening and less time talking.[1]

To conclude this book, it is worth noting that a solid and successful negotiation is like building a puzzle with several other people. The methodology I have developed and shared throughout this book has therefore been put together like a puzzle, piece by piece, step by step. Some pieces will take more time than others, some might seem more difficult to place than others; together they form a coherent whole. This approach has proven many times to be an efficient way to ensure that the negotiated agreement is put into practice, whatever the field, whether in business environments, in humanitarian or nature conservation situations, in politics, in science or in academia.

For this puzzle-building to function, there are several aspects to keep in mind throughout:

- **The other party is an opportunity:** You partner with them because you feel that by combining your resources with others, you can achieve more than you ever could alone.

- **Preparation is fundamental:** You need to know what your goal is and to understand why it is so meaningful for you; you need to think about your conditions to have many worthwhile ones. Remember that you are negotiating the conditions under which you can reach your goal, you are not negotiating your goal. Goals give energy to life and are a breeding ground for enhanced creativity. The more inspiring your goal is, the higher your motivation to reach it, and the more creative and resilient you remain. Use the **linkage tool** (page 30) to help you map your initial goal and motivations:

  o *If you could do what you wanted, what would that be?*

  o And if you do not want this situation, *what do you want instead?*

  o How will you know you have reached your goal? This question will help you find new conditions.

Research overwhelmingly shows that underprepared negotiators make unnecessary concessions, overlook potential sources of value (i.e. a variety of conditions), and very often walk away from beneficial agreements. A greater commitment to planning will improve your outcomes significantly.[2] You create things twice: first in the workshop of your mind, then in reality. When you visualize in precise details, your brain does not differentiate between fiction and reality. Project yourself into the future and imagine success. It has been proven that visualizing success helps you to attain it.

- **Believe in your aim and dare to ask.** Be courageous. Avoid situations where you say '*I gave up because I didn't dare ask*'.

- **Interest is key to success.** Interest may differ between the parties. Throughout the entire process everyone's interest needs to be taken into account for the deal to last.

- When negotiating, there are no gifts, only compensations. Negotiation dynamics are built on **exchanges**, not gifts.

- **Listening is key to success.** In a bilateral or multilateral approach a large portion of the solution comes from the other party. Your communication style must therefore remain clear, confident, open and cooperative throughout. You will need very good listening skills. Be authentic and truly interested in the other party, go with them where they take you, whilst staying focused on your goal and your ambitions. This reminds me of a sailing boat in windy weather, aiming for a specific port. At times the wind will blow the boat in a different direction, playing with the sails. But the skipper always has the end destination in mind.

- Be sharp, **concentrate**, be very aware and look for opportunities whenever there is a 'lead' from the other party.

- **Be transparent.** If the other party doesn't know what you want, they can't help you achieve it. Your goal and ambitions are your starting point and need to be communicated.

- **Emotional intelligence** is an important skill but can have a strong drawback as too much empathy can lead you to make higher concessions and to accept possibly unacceptable world views. **Social intuition**, including strong interpersonal skills and the capacity to build a trusting relationship and rapport with the other, is fundamental. This includes honesty: if something is really not possible, say so. Being sensitive to the other party's emotions is useful, even if they are putting it on, lying, pretending. Whatever they do is interesting to you as it will help you to understand them better. And most people can only fake so much.

- Keep a smile close by – after all, you can only try your best.

I hope you have enjoyed working through this book as much as I have enjoyed writing it, and that it has improved your understanding of what is required for solution-focused negotiations. I hope it will enable you to take your own negotiations to the next level.

Notes

1 Lieutenant Jack Cambria, now retired, was the longest-serving head of the New York Police Department's hostage negotiation team. K Shonk. Negotiation training with heart: A legendary hostage negotiator puts feelings first, Harvard Law School, 2018. www.pon.harvard.edu/daily/negotiation-training-daily/negotiation-training-with-heart/ (archived at https://perma.cc/E2F9-EWTV)

2 K Shonk. 5 tips for improving your negotiation skills, Harvard Law School, 2020. www.pon.harvard.edu/daily/negotiation-skills-daily/5-tips-for-improving-your-negotiation-skills/ (archived at https://perma.cc/L79A-UHZS)

BIBLIOGRAPHY

This bibliography is not exhaustive as, over the years, many different authors, speakers, customers, partners and websites have inspired my work and thoughts. The most important influence has been my actual negotiation experience and interpersonal or inter-organizational conflicts in which I have been involved. However, this bibliography provides a good basis for anyone wishing to further their knowledge and understanding of negotiation with an ethical approach regarding the other parties and with a solution-focused influence.

Amanatullah, E T and Tinsley, C H, Punishing female negotiators for asserting too much... or not enough: Exploring why advocacy moderates backlash against assertive female negotiators, *Organizational Behavior and Human Decision Processes*, 2013, 120 (1), 110–22

Bannink, F (2010) *Solution-Focused Conflict Management*, Hogrefe Publishing, Göttingen

Bertrel, L (2009) *L'essentiel de la PNL*, Jouvence, Geneva

Cain, S (2013) *Quiet: The power of introverts in a world that can't stop talking*, Broadway Books, New York

Coyle, D (2018) *The Culture Code: The secrets of highly successful groups*, Bantam Books, London

Crèvecoeur, J C (2000) *Relations et jeux de pouvoir*, Jouvence, Geneva

Crocker, C A, Hampson, F O and Aall, P (eds) (1999) *Herding Cats: Multiparty mediation in a complex world*, United States Institute of Peace Press, Washington

De Shazer, S (1985) *Keys to Solution in Brief Therapy*, Norton, New York

De Shazer, S (1988) *Clues: Investigation solutions in brief therapy*, Norton, New York

Fischer, R and Ury, W (2011) *Getting to Yes: Negotiating an agreement without giving in,* Penguin Putnam Inc, New York

Galtung, J (2004) *Transcend and Transform: An introduction to conflict work*, Pluto Press, New York

Ghazal, M (1992) *Mange ta soupe et tais-toi – une autre approche des conflits parents-enfants*, Seuil, Paris

Guidham, M (2015) *Work Communication: Mediated and face-to-face practices*, Palgrave Macmillan, London

Harvard Business Review (2000) *On Negotiation and Conflict Resolution*, Harvard Business School Press, Brighton, MA

Hoecklin, L (1995) *Managing Cultural Differences: Strategies for competitive advantage*, Addison-Wesley, Boston

Hoff, B (1983) *The Tao of Pooh*, Egmont, London

Kennedy, G (1998) *The New Negotiating Edge: The behavioural approach for results and relationships*, Nicholas Brealey, London

Kofman, F (2013) *Conscious Business*, Sounds True Inc, Boulder, CO

Kohlrieser, G (2009) *Négociations sensibles: Les techniques de négociation de prises d'otages appliquées au management*, Village Mondial

Laney, M (2002) *The Introvert Advantage: How to thrive in an extrovert world*, Workman Publishing Company, New York

Le Point, L'art de négocier, 2420, 17 January 2019

Lewis, R D (2005) *When Cultures Collide*, Nicholas Brealey, London

Lloyd Roberts, D (2006) *Staying Alive: Safety and security guidelines for humanitarian volunteers in conflict areas*, ICRC, Geneva

Mancini-Griffoli, D and Picot, A (2004) *Humanitarian Negotiation: A handbook for securing access, assistance and protection for civilians in armed conflict*, Centre for Humanitarian Dialogue, Geneva

McCormack, M H (1995) *On Negotiating*, Dove Books, London

McCormack, M H (1999) *On Communicating*, New Millennium Audio, London

Monod, J M, personal communication and interviews, (CICR), 2005.

Obama, M (2018) *Becoming*, Penguin Books Ltd, New York

O'Hanlon, B and Weiner-Davis, M (2003) *In Search of Solutions*, WW Norton & Company, New York

Patterson, K, Switzler, A, Grenny, J and McMillan, R (2012) *Crucial Conversations: Tools for talking when stakes are high*, McGraw-Hill, New York

Quéinnec, E and Igalens J (2004) *Les organisations non gouvernementales et le management*, Vuibert, Paris

Studer, F and Rosset, M (eds) (2013) *Médiation*, self-published by mediators

Toosi, N R, Semnani-Azad, Z, Shen, W, Mor, S and Amanatullah, E T (2020) How culture and race shape gender dynamics in negotiations, in *Research Handbook on Gender and Negotiation*, ed M Olekalns and J A Kennedy, Edward Elgar, Cheltenham

Ricard, M and Singer, W (2017) *Cerveau et Méditation*, Pocket, Allary Editions, Paris

Rust, S (2008) *Quand la girafe danse avec le chacal*, Editions Jouvence, Geneva

Walder, F (2003) *St-Germain ou la négociation*, Gallimard, Paris

William Zartman, I (1999) *Traditional Cures for Modern Conflicts: African conflict 'medicine'*, Lynne Rienner Publishers, Boulder, CO

Appendix

Real-life stories

In this appendix I share some real-life situations in which I have used some or all of the negotiation steps that have been presented in this book. Concrete examples will help you put into context what you have read and learned and show you how to adapt constantly to the context in which you find yourself. The examples and case studies come from various situations within business environments, not for profit organizations and academia, and have been experienced by the author. The situations have been anonymized, as most negotiations contain confidential information, and highly simplified for the purpose of this book.

This appendix provides a catalogue of examples, from finding the most useful mindset and seeing how this can be beneficial to the challenges of deciding on your goal; from being creative in discovering conditions to understanding what behaviour to adopt when meeting with others. Pick and choose the ones that are relevant to your situation or simply of interest to you. The following list should be dipped into and consulted like a dictionary, rather than read in one go as a chapter. You can work by analogy, so for example if you are aiming for a senior position somewhere, check the different points and then brainstorm what is applicable to your own situation. All the examples can be useful, whatever your topic of interest. To help you, they have been grouped into broad categories:

- employment
- supplier/purchaser
- events
- humanitarian
- personal and family

Employment

When being made redundant as an individual – can also be applied to groups

CONTEXT

Jo is an IT systems engineer. The company in which Jo[1] is employed has delocalized and outsourced the IT department's work to another country. Many colleagues will lose their jobs as labour is cheaper in the new location. The head of the IT department has called in Jo to notify them of their upcoming redundancy. Jo is informed that there will be a meeting the following week about the redundancy. This meeting will take place with the head of human resources, Jo's boss and Jo.

STEP 1: CONTEXTUAL ANALYSIS

In this step Jo needs to think about their overall goal and approach. This is important as it will influence the entire strategy to be adopted.

Being made redundant is never a pleasant experience and the outcome and finding another job may depend on how the redundancy is handled. After the initial stunned shock and feeling of unfairness and possible resentment, Jo starts thinking about what could be the best strategy for them to adopt. There are several ways in which Jo could react (which are probably not exclusive).

Jo could feel like a victim, paying the price for globalization and companies' attempts to save money by outsourcing to lower-wage countries at whatever cost. Jo would then feel hard done by, hurt (*'After all I have done for the company and for my boss'*) and simply want to hide away.

Jo might feel angry, resentful and bitter for the same reasons as above, and then would want to fight. Jo tells their friends and family bitterly how unfair it all is. Jo now simply hesitates between fighting alone, giving their boss a hard time, going to the trade union that represents the IT staff, going to the labour court or even going to find a lawyer.

Jo might decide to 'learn to surf' and to remember the saying that every problem is an opportunity in disguise. There is nothing Jo can do about the redundancy (Jo cannot change the fact that the company has decided to relocate all IT services abroad). Jo therefore decides to make the most out of the situation and to turn it into something that could be as positive as possible and be helpful. This strategy does not mean Jo is not sad, angry or disappointed. It simply means Jo will not act as a consequence of the emotions they might feel. Jo cannot stop the redundancy but Jo *can* possibly influence *the way they leave*. Jo thus opts for a more constructive approach and decides that the goal to be discussed during the meeting with the head of HR and the head of IT becomes focused on how to leave under the best conditions. This reframing of Jo's mindset will influence Jo's attitude and posture, will help them remain more in control of their emotions and will provoke a more constructive discussion with management. Jo will probably leave with more dignity and get a better deal, as the company also has an interest in avoiding social conflict and negative publicity.

Jo then goes through the contextual analysis checklist (see Chapter 4) and, where relevant (you will notice that not all topics are covered), Jo answers the questions. For instance, Jo might think about:

- *Interlocutor:* Should anyone else be present? If yes, when and how should Jo ask whether this is possible?

- *Culture:* Is there anything important to take into account with regards to the culture of the interlocutors? Even if Jo knows them as they have been working in the same company for 10 years this bears thinking about. What is also relevant here are the company's culture and the values that are communicated. Are they strong on corporate social responsibility, for instance?

- *Information to find out:* This is going to be a very important element of Jo's preparation. Jo will need to find out as much as possible about other redundancy packages in the same and in other fields, what are the legal minimum requirements, etc. Jo will also need to find out if in the past their company has had other situations where staff has been made redundant, and what the packages were then. It might also be important to find out how many other people are losing their jobs. The more information Jo can gather the better.

- *Information to give:* What is it in Jo's interest that the two heads know about them? This could include showing their knowledge about redundancy packages. Let's imagine that Jo has been made redundant before and knows that some elements can be negotiated – this might be useful information to share.

- *Planning:* Is one meeting enough or does Jo feel that there needs to be two meetings, one to discuss, then time to think and a final meeting to clinch a deal?

STEP 2: GOAL ANALYSIS
Once Jo is clear on the approach they wish to take, i.e. to make the most out of this situation, Jo then clarifies the goal and starts creating a roadmap. The roadmap could therefore look something like this (this is only a selection of possible conditions, and each one needs to be carefully thought about).

Goal: I want to leave with a good redundancy package under certain conditions.

Condition	Ambition	Limit
Financial package	6 months' salary	3 months
Outplacement programme	6 months – full programme My choice of company 100% paid by company	3 months
Job coach	6 1-hour sessions paid by company My choice of coach To start as soon as possible	
Reference letter	Me to prepare for HR and head of IT To be finalized before xx.xx.xx To be signed by xx and xx	
Reference on social media	LinkedIn reference written by head of IT Other social media	
Depending on age and country	Bridge to pension	
Pension scheme	...	
Access to training to acquire new skills *(ideally have an exact training programme in mind with facts and figures)*	Budget: 100% paid by company Time off Choice of training and organization Internal and/or external training	
Effective end date (payroll and actual)	xx.xx.xx	xx.xx.xx
Number of days per week allowed for job hunting activities (garden leave)	2 days per week	
Office equipment usage	Use own computer, phone and printer	
Computer	Jo can take on departure	
Internal vacancies	Priority access and referral letter from head of IT	
Communication of redundancy internally: when, how and by whom	xxxxx	
Communication of redundancy externally: when, how and by whom	xxxxx	
Communication of redundancy to personal contacts	Jo wants to be allowed to send emails to their network of contacts using company's email address to inform of their new email address	
Exact content of automatic email reply	Written and posted by Jo	

If you are using this for yourself, you can of course add other conditions, as with all the examples in this appendix.

STEP 3: THE ENCOUNTER

First encounter   Jo, very well prepared and thus feeling quite confident and more at peace with the decision of redundancy, goes to the scheduled meeting place and sits in a waiting room. Jo is called into the meeting room. The table is round and quite large. Jo greets both managers and sits down. Jo's entire posture is surprising to both managers, who are used to much stronger reactions and harsher facial expressions, even with some employees refusing to shake hands (pre-Covid times…). Jo waits for the meeting to start and listens carefully. And then says:

> *'I realize that the decision to relocate the IT department is non-negotiable and possibly even one that is not easy for all to accept. What I would like is then to leave under the best conditions possible, and this is what I would like to talk with you about.'*

This creates a curious and slightly surprised reaction from both managers, who tell Jo to go ahead. The ensuing dialogue could go something like this – with a calm tone of voice:

> *'As you can imagine, the situation for someone of my age is quite rough, particularly after so many years working for you. I really would like to leave on good terms. There are several things I would like to talk about with you concerning date of departure and financial aspects obviously, but also concerning support in finding a new job. Which would you like us to talk about first?'*

Let's imagine that the managers are interested primarily in the departure date. What Jo doesn't know (but guesses) is that the company is scared of adverse publicity around the decision to relocate, and worried that staff will either go on strike or take legal action. Consequences could have a high cost both for their reputation and their finance if the redundancies result in lawsuits and if circumstances change and they need to recruit new staff. On the company's roadmap, conditions may include ensuring that staff stay until the move has taken place to ensure there is no downtime for the strategic applications. They are worried that key staff, including engineers such as Jo, might leave as soon as they can, thus creating potential problems when the applications migrate to their new location. They also want the existing team to brief and train the new team.

Jo continues, confident with their ambitions which they believe in.

'Ideally I would be paid for 6 months and my final day would be xx.xx.xxxx. If you wish, I could leave earlier than the official date. As there are three years left before I am entitled to retire, I would really appreciate if the company would help bridge those years to my pension plan. How does that sound to you?'

You will note how Jo brings in some important conditions, including two vital ones, in a conversational way, indicating *this is my wish, let's discuss.* Depending on what the company has decided, reactions might be positive, needing more information, or curious about other requests. Let's imagine the following response from human resources (HR):

HR: *'Asking for 6 months' pay is quite steep. What we offer is 3 months' pay with some outplacement help.'*

Jo: *'Well I know that 6 months might seem steep to you but I do know that it is possible – many companies do offer better financial packages than the minimum legal one[2] and in this case I really think that 6 months is not unreasonable. I am glad you mentioned outplacement. I would really appreciate some help and assistance in finding a new job. It would be great if I could have 6 months' outplacement programme and I would like to be able to choose with which company. Would that be possible?'*

HR: *'We have already made a careful selection of outplacement companies. HR can give you the list. The programme we could offer is the 3 month full one.'*

Jo: *'If I go for one of the outplacement companies you suggest and for the 3 month programme when I really hoped for the 6 month one, could I have access to a specialized job coach? With my age and qualifications this might prove really useful. I know that when people are made redundant there is usually the possibility of having time for looking for employment. I am not sure what you have planned but 2 full days a week would be good for me.'*

HR's response depends on their exact roadmap:

'If we give you 2 days a week garden leave, i.e. time off to do other things such as hunt for a new job or be coached, we would like to plan them so that the rest of the time we can count on you training X and Y...'

And so on, going through the conditions, stating the ambitions, checking the response and moving forward. The posture is one of request and confidence, as Jo knows that the managers are their best opportunity, as do the HR and IT heads. The communication style is open and cooperative yet firm and clear. HR and IT are fully aware they need Jo and that Jo knows what is being asked for is reasonable.

Depending on the time left in the meeting, a second encounter might be decided. Jo will send an email outlining everything that was discussed (being conscious that they were discussed, not formally agreed).

STEP 4: THE OFFER

Jo goes through the steps involved in building an offer, even though Jo is aware that the offer will most probably come from HR. Let's imagine the following happened:

Conditions	Ambitions	Reaction (other)	Limits
Financial package	6 months' salary	3 months is what is offered. Company may be open to the idea if Jo will sign a confidentiality agreement	3 months
Outplacement programme	6 months – full programme	3 months full programme	3 months
	My choice of company	Company has a list to be chosen from	
	100% paid by company	Yes	
Job coach	6 one-hour sessions paid by company	4 – no need for more as outplacement programme offered	
	My choice of coach	Yes	
	To start as soon as possible	Yes as soon as everything has been agreed to	
Reference letter	Me to prepare for HR and head of IT	Yes	
	To be finalized before xx.xx.xx	Will be done the week before the final day	
	To be signed by xx and xx	Yes	

(continued)

(Continued)

Conditions	Ambitions	Reaction (other)	Limits
Reference on social media	LinkedIn reference written by head of IT	No	
	Other social media	No. Only LinkedIn is officially used by company	
Bridge to pension	Full	Possible 80% if Jo doesn't find a new job	
Access to training for diploma X	100% paid by company	Yes for diploma X which is 12 days' training. Jo to pay F&B and transport, company to pay for training	
	Time off	Yes so long as training days become garden leave days, i.e. 2 days off a week to be planned	
	Choice of training and organization	Done	
Effective end date (payroll and actual)	xx.xx.xx	Yes, so long as Jo stays on until the end. This can be reviewed as soon as Jo's replacement has been trained. A special contractual clause needs to be signed	
Number of days per week allowed for job-hunting activities	2 days per week	Yes (see above)	
Office equipment usage	Use own computer, phone and printer	Yes	
Computer	Jo can take on departure	Someone needs to clean the computer and remove all applications and company data	
Internal vacancies	Priority access and referral letter from head of IT	(Was never talked about)	
Communication of redundancy	Internal and external by xxxx and all communications written by Jo	Head of IT and HR will send an email by xxx.xxx to all company staff – Jo can check content of email and make recommendations if wanted. These may or not be followed. Jo can prepare a mailing to contacts giving new email address	

Jo is satisfied because, compared to the initial package, a lot more has been achieved. The only ambition that requires compensation is the reference on LinkedIn. Here Jo will try to compensate with the possibility of posting part of the reference letter on Jo's LinkedIn page.

The offer – if made by Jo – would look something like:

If you, company X:

- give me 6 months' pay
- bridge pension if no other employment is secured
- agree to final date xx.xx.xx
- give me 2 days a week garden leave
- pay me to go to a full outplacement programme for 3 months
- pay for job coaching session up to £/hour for 4 sessions
- …

Then I will ensure I will:

- leave only at the end of my contract
- organize a departure drinks party and invite the two of you (to indicate goodwill)
- guarantee full confidentiality of this agreement
- train future replacement
- plan to work 3 days a week and ensure work is done to the same standard as usual
- document project x and y
- document processes x and y
- avoid contact with trade union and journalists
- …

STEP 5: THE IMPLEMENTATION

During the final encounter, a schedule for making out the contract will have been discussed, together with arranging dates for various items that were discussed such as reference letter and internal communication.

The above is based on a real story, which finished with a final drinks party and the CEO saying to Jo they had rarely see someone leave with so little anger and bitterness, and stay so professional to the end.

Example of a roadmap with conditions when negotiating a leadership position

This example is for a position in science[3] although many conditions can apply to any professional environment. This example can also be used, adapted, to look for a new job.

You are a senior scientist looking for a group leader position so that you can set up your own lab and carry out your cutting edge research. Your strategy will be twofold. First you will concentrate on where and in what kind of environment you want to work, and second when you have found the university, institute or pharmaceutical company (or other company) you will focus on the job conditions.

You can also use this roadmap and conditions, slightly adapted, if you are a PhD looking for a postdoc position. You do not as yet have a geographic preference. As with the group leader situation, you might have two separate roadmaps – one for your own usage to reflect and help you decide where you want to do your postdoc, the other for the actual negotiation of the position.

STEP 1: CONTEXTUAL ANALYSIS

The first thing you need to do is decide where you would like to carry out your research. You might decide on a list of elements that are important for you, first concentrating on overall conditions pertaining to the choice of university, institute or pharmaceutical company. Here you have an interesting choice to make, depending on your personal situation: what is most important to you, the city you live in or your research? In other words, do you base your search on the country/geographical location you wish to live in and then select the organization/university/company from what is available, or do you first choose the organization/university/company and thus the geographical location is secondary? Your answer will most probably depend on your personal situation, and can be a (very) difficult choice when your partner is, for instance, in one city/country and your ideal research institute is in another. You will need to think about the following (amongst others):

- choice of university or company: which institute, university, pharmaceutical company or start-up, international organization, company
- reputation and specialization (area of research)
- mission and values

- field
- available facilities
- for universities, numbers of publications
- size (number of staff, admin, scientists)
- country
- city
- time travelling to work
- languages spoken – international environment
- grant opportunities (national funding, EU, etc)
- parking or public transport possibilities
- ...

You will probably go through your contextual analysis quite quickly, as once you have chosen the university you would like to join you may not have much choice about the people with whom you will be negotiating.

Planning, cultural aspects and information will need to be carefully thought about and prepared. The initial encounters will take place online, but you would like at least one site visit to see the campus and facilities available.

STEP 2: GOAL ANALYSIS

Once you have chosen where you would like to work, your goal will be one of the following (depending on where you are in your career):

- I want a group leader position to set up my lab under certain conditions.
- I want the best postdoc position under certain conditions.
- I want a good job under certain conditions.

You then elaborate a roadmap with regards to the specific position and lab requirements for your research. This is the roadmap you will use in the interviews and negotiations. Conditions can be grouped into families and most of them will need to be further broken down and fine-tuned. Each will have an ambition and some a limit.

Position conditions:

- position and title
- responsibilities

- evolution and career perspectives
- type of contract
- percentage employment rate
- flexible percentage and home working possibilities
- detailed job description
- to whom you report
- which committees you want to be part of
- salary
- allowances for lunch/cafeteria
- start date
- pension planning
- medical insurance
- overtime compensation
- holidays
- unpaid leave if required or requested
- projects to be part of/involved in
- networks to be actively part of or informed about
- budget for lab retreats
- conferences: time allowed, choice of conference, organizational aspects
- training opportunities (soft, technical and hard skills) for self and for team
- travel funding (including funds to attend conferences)
- presence off site/in lab
- teaching duties percentage
- teaching language
- help in looking for funding partners and writing grant applications
- time for grant application/help with grant application
- admin time percentage
- access to secretary/administrative help
- skills I want to use/develop
- meeting with management – what regularity, with whom

- management/team leader position, number of people, profile of people
- meet team before signing
- how my recruitment/position is communicated
- ...

Lab conditions (for the group leader position):

- start-up money/package
- space size of office
- space size of lab
- lab location (in which building)
- office location
- number of desks
- number of benches
- number of high benches
- lights (ceiling and bench)
- access to computers
- access to specialized equipment
- other special needs
- team members to recruit: postdocs, PhDs, lab technicians, administrative help
- right to decide who to recruit
- HR help with recruitment
- HR help with work permits/visa applications
- secretary/administrative help
- specific lab equipment, including medical or technical devices, other facilities
- access to IT/computational biology/core services support
- IP rights
- ...

Postdoc conditions (for the postdoc position):

- freedom of project topic

- time for own research
- time for supervision
- publishing quota
- ...

Relocating conditions:

- help with finding job for partner/spouse
- childcare
- housing – help with finding accommodation
- housing – financial help
- help with visa/work permit application
- relocation budget and assistance
- partner support
- insurances
- ...

Other:

- language courses
- parking
- maternity/paternity leave
- ...

It may be that you answer a call and are offered a package. As always, it is in your best interest to 'set the package aside' and go up one level into your ego bubble so that you are not simply reacting to an offer but thinking about you and what the ideal contract would look like. Obviously the values of your ambitions will depend on the university or company and country. Remember, you need to believe in your ambitions, mention them and fight for them.

STEP 3: THE ENCOUNTER

Whether online or in physical presence, the encounters are your opportunity to discuss your needs and wishes, to be clear on what you would like and to listen to the other party's needs, wishes and concerns. The more you listen, the more you will find out, and possibly be able to use that knowledge.

STEP 4: THE OFFER

The offer will be made by the university or company. Make sure the implementation conditions have been discussed and agreed to before anything is signed.

STEP 5: THE IMPLEMENTATION

See above.

Example of an introductory statement when transitioning from a temporary to a permanent position

What follows is an example of an introductory statement that can be made to HR when seeking a permanent position. Whilst the example is derived from a real situation in the scientific field, it can be used in any area of activity.

You are a postdoc working on a project that is taking place jointly in a lab in your university and in a large pharmaceutical company. Your project is giving promising results and the publication date is soon. The pharmaceutical company has verbally mentioned to you several times the possibility of offering you a permanent position. Until now the discussions have only been verbal and you really need some official commitment as you will otherwise need to start looking for another job.

STEP 1: CONTEXTUAL ANALYSIS

First of all you need to prepare your contextual analysis, answering the following questions:

- Who is your best interlocutor? In this case it could be the head of HR or the head of R&D.
- What is their power of decision/influence?
- What information can you gather about them, including cultural information and communication preferences?
- What is the best way to contact them?
- What information – if any – do you think they should have prior to the meeting?
- How would you like the meeting to take place – virtual or in presence, in the lab or in an office?
- …

The more you prepare the context the better, even though you need to keep open to surprises.

STEP 2: GOAL ANALYSIS

You then prepare your roadmap with the goal: I want a permanent position under certain conditions. Conditions will include many of the ones in the previous example.

STEP 3: THE ENCOUNTER

Third, you prepare your introductory statement. The introductory statement you could use in your meeting with HR or with the head of R&D might be the following (this is an example; adapt it to your own language):

> *'I am planning my next career steps as we will soon finish the project and publish the results. I really would like to continue working for you in a permanent position. This has been discussed with my boss several times. As I need to have a firm commitment, what would need to happen for you to be able to onboard me and give me a written offer? What would the process be?'*

And you enter into the core part of the encounter. You first listen to your interlocutor's reply and observe their reaction, and then you seek conversational opportunities to discuss your conditions whilst listening carefully to their concerns, needs and wishes. Remember, you are focusing on what it will take for you to get this permanent position, not on arguing why you should be given it. It is often a good idea at the end of an encounter to send an email thanking them for their time and summarizing the main points that were discussed.

Supplier/purchaser

Example of negotiating a contract with a new supplier

You work in a large non-governmental organization (NGO) involved with internally displaced people. There is a need to install and deploy a donor management (DM) software. You have been asked to find the best software for the organization. You decide to proceed in two steps.

First you need to get the exact specifications pertaining to the technical aspects and to the functionalities internally and write them up in the format of a roadmap with conditions, ambitions and limits. Then you will list the criteria you find important for selecting a supplier, such as size of company, track record with NGOs, geographical location of support team, language spoken, number of customers who have bought this software, etc. These could be called 'supplier conditions', which you will use for the initial short-list of companies you will contact.

When you have made your selection of potential suppliers, you will then map out and send your specifications, most probably in the format of a request for information (RFI) or request for proposal (RFP). The difference with more traditional ways of choosing a new software/supplier is that you have limits *and* ambitions. Usually when people think about their software and user requirements they put one value only, as in for instance 'language=English' or 'response time for help screen=6 seconds'. When there is only one value specified, this value often represents your limit, i.e. a response time of 6 seconds means that you do not want response time for the users to be longer than 6 seconds. In the situation presented here, you think about your ideal response time first. For instance your ideal response time (i.e. your ambition) may be 2 seconds, and any response time longer than 6 seconds is unacceptable. This will enable you to communicate and try to reach your ideal, and, if not possible, to compensate any movement away from your ambition (see Chapter 10).

Finally, when you have received various responses and made your choice, you will then negotiate the terms of the contract to buy the software.

STEP 1: CONTEXTUAL ANALYSIS
In this example you will not necessarily need to carry out a contextual analysis.

STEP 2: GOAL ANALYSIS
Once you have selected your supplier, you will carefully elaborate your roadmap. Once again, conditions can be grouped in families for more clarity and creativity. The families in this context might be:

- object conditions, which are related to the product or the service
- relationship with supplier conditions, which relates to the relationship you would like to have with the supplier
- contractual conditions, anything linked with the contract

This could give you a roadmap looking something like this (the conditions will need to be carefully broken down into more details):

Goal: I want to buy the best donor management software under certain conditions.

Object conditions:

- conditions linked with the DM functionalities: tracking donors, history of what has been given, how much, how and when; prospect tracking; accounting; contact and communication tracking…
- conditions pertaining to technical aspects, installation and deployment: what language will the users be able to use; speed of response; code used; where will the data be stored; how many servers; technical training needed; customizing requirements; capacity to transfer current data (and not have to re-enter information); need to have local database administrators
- …

Relationship with supplier conditions:

- a single point of contact or a single key account manager
- regular meetings during implementation stage (how often, when, where, with whom)
- problem-solving process
- training needs and possibilities (technical and user functionalities)
- a technical team that stays the same until full deployment
- after-sales service
- maintenance and regular update
- project management methodology
- escalation process in case of delay or other problems
- training of internal technical staff
- user training
- …

Contractual conditions:

- pricing and financial conditions: software, licencing, customizing, implementation, deployment, training, new modules, upgrades
- planning and dates: signature, start of project, delivery of modules, pilot, 'go live'
- insurances
- back-up plans
- …

STEP 3: THE ENCOUNTER

These may vary between online and site visit. Your introductory statement could be: '*We would like to buy this software and would like to discuss the conditions under which we could work together.*'

Because of the nature of the subject, buying and selling, talking about conditions will seem more natural than in some other examples. Once again, make sure you use open language, ensuring that you remain flexible on certain values and that under certain conditions you might be willing to move. You keep moving forward, remembering you never commit during an encounter.

STEP 4: THE OFFER

In this step you will analyse what has been discussed during the encounters and clarify your offer:

> '*If you are willing to install software X by xx.xx.xx, for a cost of...,*
> *if you name a key account manager for us who speaks English and is*
> *available within 24 hours of receiving a question, if you ...., then*
> *we will make sure you receive a down payment of xx by xx.xx.xx, we*
> *will pay yearly for 120 licences, we will provide you with technical*
> *information pertaining to the existing database and will name an*
> *internal IT specialist to be dedicated to this project...*'

STEP 5: THE IMPLEMENTATION

Some of the elements you will have decided with the supplier may include by when the legal aspects will be confirmed, when the initial project kick-off will take place, and when and with what frequency you will have status meetings.

Events

Example of organizing a concert or other entertainment events

You are a university student who volunteers regularly for an NGO. You strongly believe in an environmental conservation project they run linked with solar powered portable stoves. With a group of like-minded friends you decide that you would like to do something concrete to help with this project and you decide to organize a concert to help raise funds. Your idea is to have a large public that is made up of families and adults as well as young people, which is why you would like to organize several bands playing from mid-afternoon to late night.

STEP 1: CONTEXTUAL ANALYSIS

In this step you will analyse the overall context, including several negotiations you might wish to have. You might want to talk to potential funders, to commercial partners, and obviously to the bands and to the venue people.

STEP 2: GOAL ANALYSIS

The following roadmap includes your overall strategic plan, which then will need to be fine-tuned and adapted. Once again – like in the above example to select a supplier – there are several levels of determining conditions: the first level is to help decide and choose the venue and the bands. The second level will be linked to the actual contractual conditions to be negotiated.

Your overall goal will be: we want to organize a concert for NGO X under certain conditions. You then analyse what exactly this means for you.

You might wish to group the conditions into families. These can include the following.

Conditions linked with the venue:

- location (city, neighbourhood)
- size of venue (number of seats)
- size of stage
- backstage commodities
- separate entrance for performers
- fan zone area
- general access facilities
- lodges and facilities for performers
- bar amenities
- cost of venue
- security aspects
- …

Conditions linked to the bands and musicians:

- groups to be asked
- price/fee for musicians

- payment conditions
- hotel and food and beverages for the musicians
- transport
- date and time for the gig and for the sound check
- contract signature date
- insurance/cancellation conditions
- equipment requirements
- choice of songs
- length of gig
- number of encores
- recording and filming rights
- ...

Conditions linked to ticketing and planning:

- number of tickets
- cost per ticket
- sales channels
- reimbursement conditions
- paper or electronic ticketing
- start date for selling tickets
- how many VIP tickets
- ...

Conditions pertaining to communication and PR:

- choice of media: posters, flyers, online only
- social networks
- website: musicians, NGO
- budget
- interviews (radio, newspaper, TV) with NGO, with bands
- fan zone treat
- ...

STEP 3: THE ENCOUNTERS

Each family of conditions will probably give rise to a roadmap, which will be the topic of the encounters. With the venue people, for instance, your introductory statement will be '*We would like to organize a concert in your venue and wish to discuss the conditions under which this might be possible.*' With the band, '*We would like to organize a concert for this NGO and would like you to be the lead band. We would like to discuss this project further with you.*' The rule remains: you state what you would like and open to discuss the conditions on both sides.

Humanitarian

Example linked with negotiating access to prisoners in a humanitarian context

You work for an organization that is involved in human rights and primarily with detention conditions for prisoners of war that have been arrested and detained for political reasons. Your organization has asked you to visit a selection of prisons in country X. For this you need to be very careful to have all the correct authorizations. You are planning a discussion with the government official who is in charge of the country's prisons and detention camps. You require the proper authorization, and you also have certain requirements, such as to be able to talk with prisoners in a safe and confidential environment.

STEP 1: CONTEXTUAL ANALYSIS

A highly simplified contextual analysis could look like this:

Aim (macro level): I want to gain access to prisoners in various detention centres in country Z			
	Desired conditions (what I really would like)	**Known elements**	**Unacceptable conditions**
Interlocutor: name, function, power/ influence...	Mr X, chief of government department responsible for prisons, and Ms Y, prison governor of Z	Mr X was educated in UK. New in this position but was a police officer before this role. Ms Y...	

(continued)

(Continued)

Cultural aspects to bear in mind, (e.g. possible need for interpreter)	Mr X is part of tribe A and speaks perfect English as was educated in UK. Ms Y is part of tribe B. Her English is ok but local interpreter may be needed	Tribe A people are known to be very (straightforward, shy, authoritarian...)	
Timing, planning and possible deadlines	Meetings online and at least one in-person visit to the country. Meetings to be planned by end June and to take place before end September	Elections will take place in November so all must be signed before September and visits planned before...	Agreement to visits must be made before September (and next elections)
Location and access	Capital city X with access to the main prison there. Online meetings possible	Visa is needed to visit country X and valid 3 months	Not possible (budget) to travel to country more than 3 times
Logistical and security issues	Safe and quiet environment for the meetings. Confidentiality to be ensured, nothing to be recorded. Only minutes will be shared	Government offices are noisy and not secured or air-conditioned	People armed in the meetings is not acceptable
My team: who, what roles, any need for experts, what authority	I will be with my colleague M, who will act as co-pilot. Human rights experts to be available		I will not go alone. Interpreter chosen by me
Communication style and media used	Initial meeting should be in presence. Email to keep track and send summaries. Check what videoconference facilities are available. Check communication style linked to culture and who is to receive summaries		
Information: to find out, to ask, to give	Get more info on culture of tribe and on previous visits to prisons. Tell them of my experience		

STEP 2: GOAL ANALYSIS

You will then elaborate your roadmap. Some of the conditions you want to talk about and achieve include the following:

- Access to which prisoners: political prisoners? Male/female prisoners? Adult/juvenile?
- Access to what category of prisoner: condemned, parole?
- Location of detention (prisons, camps, hospitals, police centres)
- Calendar: how long in advance do the visits need to be planned, when can they take place?
- Duration of the visits
- What you can bring to the prisoner
- What you can communicate to the prisoner's family/external world
- Access to and choice of interpreter
- Who will be present to the visits (ideally alone with prisoners with no prison staff present, only interpreter when necessary)
- Confidentiality of the content of the discussions and of the actual visit
- Recording of the visits
- Relationship with director of detention centre/prison: what information to share, how often to meet, location, duration
- Communication of (anonymized) situations

Your (again highly simplified) roadmap could look like this:

Goal: I want to be able to visit prisoners in prison X		
Conditions	**Ambitions**	**Limit**
Access to prisoners	NGO to be allowed to decide: Male and female in similar proportion Condemned or paroled Adults and minors	If prison or government decide unilaterally
How to determine who and gain access	NGO to present a list to government for validation	

(continued)

(Continued)

Deadline for government response	4 weeks after reception of the list	
Who will take part in the visits	NGO officials only with their interpreter	No prison officials allowed
Location of visits	NGO premises Prisoner brought by prison officials who will wait outside during the visit	In the visiting room of prison with doors and windows open
Feedback of visits	Total anonymity by NGO Official rapport to be anonymized and given to govt, prison officials, NGO management and Amnesty international	
Gifts/packages to prisoner	NGO to be able to bring food, books or health/medical items, letters, phones, money	
Communication	NGO to be allowed to reassure family of prisoners If prisoner wants to phone family, OK for a 5 minute call Prisoner allowed to give letter to family members to be posted by NGO	If prison officials read letter
Food and drinks	Snacks and water/tea to be available and allowed	

Example linked with setting up a refugee camp

You work for a large humanitarian organization and are involved in a project to set up a refugee camp following a natural disaster.

First you need to talk with government officials about the actual need to have a camp and about the necessary requirements to set one up. You will also need to talk with other NGOs to ensure that aid is coordinated, as well as with the local communities that live around the area where the future camp will be to ensure their support. Financial partners will also need to be taken into account.

In many complex situations like this one there will be several levels of reflections to be had:

- high-level (strategic)
- operational
- ground (frontline)

Each one leads to one or more roadmaps and project management approaches. The list of conditions below will help plan at a high level what needs to be thought about. Most probably work groups will then tackle individual topics and create their own very specific roadmap, such as '*I want an adequate medical system in place under certain conditions*', and the specific conditions will be outlined. Or '*I want a solid admin team to be able to work comfortably under certain conditions*', and there again the exact conditions will need to be clarified.

STEP 1: CONTEXTUAL ANALYSIS

In your contextual analysis you will need to carefully map your stakeholders and your interlocutors, understanding their various spheres of influence: to decide, to be experts, to agree… A detailed contextual analysis for each one may be necessary.

STEP 2: GOAL ANALYSIS

Your overall goal will be: I want to set up a refugee camp under certain conditions.

The conditions, grouped into families, can include (these will need to be carefully fine-tuned) the following.

Location and access conditions:

- exact location where the camp should be created
- number of refugees (individuals and families) that will be accepted
- who draws plans, who validates them
- size of camp including living quarters, amenities, space per family/per individual
- amenities: latrines, sleeping quarters, medical centres, dispensary, child-care…
- geographical coverage from which refugees can come from
- freedom of movement for refugees within the camp
- ease of access from capital, major city
- …

Conditions related to assistance for staff, for refugees:

- health – number of doctors, nurses; necessary equipment, medication, dispensary size, beds...
- administration work – how many people, what skills, size of offices, equipment
- legal help for refugees
- sports and other activities, pitch, equipment
- language lessons
- childcare area and support, staff, toys and other equipment
- basic schooling, classroom, number of children/adults, teachers
- ...

Basic necessities conditions:

- food and storage
- water – construction of wells possible
- toilets, showers and washing facilities
- small shop for regular needs
- postal service
- ...

Protection and security conditions:

- camp protection
- access issues to enter the camp and various offices, areas
- planning conditions
- project management team
- dates and milestones
- budget
- roles and responsibilities
- ...

Conditions linked to communication: how, by when, by who, using what means:

- with stakeholders
- with local communities

- with government
- with other international organizations and NGOs
- with refugees
- ...

Conditions linked with funding and other resources:

- accounting
- who is responsible for budget
- who decides/signs
- fundraising
- ...

Conditions linked to cost of rental/buying land:

- expertise to be done
- ownership of land
- cost
- ...

Governing body of camp:

- team
- stakeholders' rights
- ...

STEP 3: THE ENCOUNTERS

Obviously you will have many encounters, which will take place with all the potential stakeholders, at times bilaterally and when necessary in multi-partite meetings. It is very important to involve stakeholders as early as possible so that they support the camp, or at least don't damage the project. Agreements reached through coercion seldom lead to durable arrangements on the frontline, because they are often contested. Depending on the situation of the country in which you need to build this refugee camp, you might need to talk to armed groups, government officials, local communities and land owners, civilians, UN agencies, any NGO or international organization that already work in this country/location, private donors and other funding agencies, your own NGO, the core team, etc.

Personal and family

Example linked with discussing (negotiating) online time with
a teenager – mindset, linkage and goal

You currently live with your two teenagers at home. In your opinion they spend a lot of time online, mainly on social networks and playing games. Many conflicts arise because you try to set rules that are hard to enforce and because they do not understand why you get so fed up. It has become a constant, regular source of contention. You are distraught because you find the situation unhealthy and because you are worried about their attitude towards being online constantly (as it seems to you). You have not only noticed that their homework is suffering, but also the family atmosphere has deteriorated and they rarely go out to play or do sports. Your initial reaction as a parent is '*I am fed up. I don't want my children to be glued non-stop to their mobile phone.*'

If you follow this line of thought your reaction will tend to be either convincing or pleading: '*Please don't do this, please be more careful of family moments together…*', or possibly aggressive and fed up: '*I am fed up to the back teeth with your gaming, now put your phone down*'. If, however, you decide to try the approach outlined in this book, remember the golden rule: you need the other party (your teenagers) in order to get what you want. Even if you are fed up, and possibly rightly so, they are your best opportunity. The second golden rule is that your goal is something you want for yourself *and not something you do not want the other person to do.* You might find it helpful to use the linkage tool (see Chapter 3) and to ask yourself the question '*Why don't I want my children to be glued to their mobile phones?*' This will fill the top part of the linkage tool and help you frame your goal in a more positive way. Your next question will be, '*If I do not want them to be glued to their mobile phones, what do I want instead?*'

If you communicate what you don't want, you risk entering in a possibly sterile discussion and argument, ending more often than not in a feeling of frustration and misunderstanding (teenagers thinking that the generation gap is too wide for you to understand, that you are always telling them what to do…).

If, however, you turn your goal into something positive that you would like to achieve, using what you have thought about and written in the top of your linkage tool, the following discussion and negotiation will tend to be more productive. Remember, as you need the other party to get what you want – this is also a negotiation after all – your teenagers need to become your partners rather than your enemies, and to be involved from the start. Your goal could therefore become something like ' I want a balanced and healthy family under certain conditions.'

The ensuing discussion will focus on what it means for everyone to be a healthy and balanced family. Enjoy being creative, which will not be possible with the goal '*I do not want you to spend so much time on mobile phones.*' Keep in mind that views *will differ but need to be listened to and understood* if you want to have a constructive discussion that may possibly lead to a more peaceful family life. Otherwise you will probably continue with the daily struggle, or you will simply impose rules that are hard to enforce.

The following conditions might be discussed with your children:

- time spent together doing family activities (sports, cultural or outdoor activities)
- time spent offline for all members of the family
- time spent doing homework
- time spent watching films/TV
- time for social networks and gaming – free time online
- what kind of online activities
- eating together with no phone or tablet on the table for parents and teenagers alike
- inviting friends to come over
- budget for external activities
- ...

Although not a recipe for immediate and definite success, approaching the situation in this manner might well lead to a more constructive discussion than a blank '*I don't want you to do what you want to do.*' It also helps contextualize and explain the issue, whereby you can also explain your worry (see Chapter 7 on non-violent communication). Be aware that you must also be willing to change your own habits and accept being offline and not checking your emails at any moment of the day.

Some useful tips when negotiating with children and teenagers:

- Distinguish clearly what is negotiable and what is non-negotiable – first in your mind then with the others – and ensure that both parents share the same goal and agree on what is negotiable and non-negotiable. You will have to communicate this clearly, expressing what you want (and not what you don't want).

- Practise active listening, and really seek to understand their point of view, *making it obvious you want to learn and understand how they see things.* Keep in mind that their worldview is not necessarily yours. You might need to adapt your language. Consciously keep the tone of voice and discussion cooperative, once again seek to be curious not furious, to listen, to understand not to react, remembering at all times that their reality and needs are not necessarily the same as yours.

- Be flexible and coherent.

- Make sure you have sufficient time and be patience – their schedule and willingness to talk does not necessarily fit yours.

- Avoid using your parental power to impose until all other avenues have been explored, and never take them for fools.

Notes

1 Jo is a fictitious name.

2 Jo is showing that they know their stuff and have done their research on the topic.

3 K Weston and J Roostlau (2018) *A Career in Research*, Wellcome. https://wellcome.org/sites/default/files/research-careers-tips-running-research-group-2018-05-17.pdf (archived at https://perma.cc/EPY6-LSA9)

INDEX

NB: page numbers in *italic* indicate figures or tables.

CPSIA information can be obtained
at www.ICGtesting.com
Printed in the USA
BVHW010948100423
662058BV00012B/178

9 781398 601802